- Pint-Sized Poets Vol II

Edited by Lynsey Hawkins

First published in Great Britain in 2006 by:
Young Writers
Remus House
Coltsfoot Drive
Peterborough
PE2 9JX
Telephone: 01733 890066
Website: www.youngwriters.co.uk

SB ISBN 1 84602 395 5

Foreword

Young Writers was established in 1991 and has been passionately devoted to the promotion of reading and writing in children and young adults ever since. The quest continues today. Young Writers remains as committed to the fostering of burgeoning poetic and literary talent as ever.

This year's Young Writers competition has proven as vibrant and dynamic as ever and we are delighted to present a showcase of the best poetry from across the UK. Each poem has been carefully selected from a wealth of *Playground Poets* entries before ultimately being published in this, our thirteenth primary school poetry series.

Once again, we have been supremely impressed by the overall high quality of the entries we have received. The imagination, energy and creativity which has gone into each young writer's entry made choosing the best poems a challenging and often difficult but ultimately hugely rewarding task - the general high standard of the work submitted amply vindicating this opportunity to bring their poetry to a larger appreciative audience.

We sincerely hope you are pleased with our final selection and that you will enjoy *Playground Poets - Pint-Sized Poets Vol II* for many years to come.

Contents

SS Peter & Paul's Catholic Primary School, St Helens

Strathburn School, Inverurie

The Poems

Listen

Listen!
What can you hear?
Shiny, brown conkers fall from oak trees
And spiky, brown hedgehogs hibernate.
Bright green leaves turn to orange, red and yellow.
Children wear woolly hats and scarves.
Long turn to short days.
People sit by fires and drink hot chocolate.

Listen!
What can you hear?
Trees do a special dance in the wind
And leaves crunch under people's feet.
Squirrels looking for juicy berries to eat for the winter.
Gardeners are busy collecting flowers.

Tyla Danskin (6)

Leo

He watches over his domain
Where his species will forever reign.

The burning heat of the blazing sun
Is no match for the wild one.

His Royal Highness prowls on the hunt
Waiting to pull the majestic stunt.

Patiently listening for the moment to strike
This crucial moment is the difference between
Starvation and life.

Megan Crossley (9)

Winter

Sitting down while snow is brewing
Everyone stops what they are doing
Snug and cosy, watching telly
But not poor Mum, she's making jelly
We all gather around the Christmas tree
Opening pressies for you and me
Yes, yes, it's time for the roast
Let's hope I get the most
Hooray! Hooray! It's Christmas Eve
I wish that Santa would never leave.

Lucy Powell (10)

My Nan Is Great

My nan is
The best because
She is so fun
To be with.

At night
She takes
Her teeth
Out and
Becomes toothless
But my nan
Is so funny.

She is the
Best nan in
The world
And no one can
Be funnier than
Her!

Sophia Cox (11)
Beck Primary School, Sheffield

What Is Pink?

(Based on 'What is Pink?' by Christina Rosetti)

What is pink?
A pig is pink snorting at the farm.

What is blue?
The sea is blue waving at the beach.

What is red?
A rose is red growing in the garden.

What is white?
Clouds are white floating in the air.

What is orange?
Fire is orange flaming at firework shows.

What is green?
Grass is green blowing on the ground.

What is yellow?
The sun is yellow shining in the sky.

Keziah Saunders (7)
Beck Primary School, Sheffield

My Love

When it's dark the moon reflects off the sun
To give the light we need
But when the sun doesn't want to do its job
You come to comfort me
'Cause you're my star that gives me light in the dark
'Cause you're my sunshine
And the light that you bring
'Cause you stand by me
But when the years went by
Her spirit began to drift away
So I was left alone
So I wanted to drift away
To love you in Heaven.

Kyle Newton (11)
Beck Primary School, Sheffield

Mountain Depths

In the mountain depths, way up in the sky
The mountains creep up high
The mountains, misty and cold
The mountains, graceful and bold

In the mountains, really high
I'm going to try and get to the top
I guess I have to try.

Joshua Bamford (10)
Beck Primary School, Sheffield

The Ocean Waves

The sea has many mysteries
And the ocean waves are one
They combine together
To stay not alone!
Climb and fall against the rocks
Then they stumble back into the rapid sea
One by one they do their best to succeed
But they fail
And go back in the sea in shame.

Jade Reilly (10)
Beck Primary School, Sheffield

My Mum

My mum is as bouncy as a kangaroo
Her hair is as soft as cotton wool
She is as happy as a clown
Her eyes are as brown as a bear's fur
She is so energetic like a monkey swinging in the trees.

Lauren Holmes (11)
Beck Primary School, Sheffield

Deep Sea

Deep on the bottom of the ocean,
Strange fish, never seen before, swim.
Eels swim fiercely across the seabed,
While the plankton float around lazily.
The sun's rays cannot reach this deep, dark world.
Higher, the big fishes live and never sleep.
Sharks swim slowly eyeing over fish,
Small schools of fish swim swiftly.
Mythical creatures roam around destroying anything in their path.

Lewis Waddingham (10)
Beck Primary School, Sheffield

My Mum

My mum is a twinkling
Star in the sky

My mum smells as
Beautiful as a rose

My mum looks as
Pretty as a bunch of flowers

My mum works as
Hard as slaves

My mum is a paradise city.

Alice Green (10)
Beck Primary School, Sheffield

Horse

My horse is very kind to people
Because it gets played with.
My horse is beautiful like a star.
It is as beautiful as the midnight sky.
My horse has a tail as shiny as a bird's wing.

Chantelle Speight (11)
Beck Primary School, Sheffield

The Flowers

Flowers are shining in the sun.
Some are yellow, gold and even purple.
When you water them they grow right up to the sky.
Some of them glow like the sun, some blow like the wind.
People try to stand on them but they run away.
The roses are red to light up your garden.
Sunflowers are high, they reach the sky.
They attract bees.
Daisies are so bright they glow.
Lilies are so bright they glow like the sun.
All flowers are so pretty that you can stare at them all day long.
Flowers glow, so do you.

Abbie Simmons (10)
Beck Primary School, Sheffield

The Night Is Dark And The Sky Is Blue

The night is dark
And the stars are
Twinkling in the night sky
And the moon
Shines brightly in the
Dark night sky.
The sky is blue.
The sky is blue
And the red-hot sun
Shines on the dry lilies
And the people play
In their swimming pool
While the red-hot sun
shines on the gleaming water.

Kirsty Hiley (11)
Beck Primary School, Sheffield

Ultimate Car

From my bedroom window I see a blur suddenly
Like a Subaru with nitrous gas that has been pulled and pushed
Down an enormous runway.
It is so colourful like a rainbow
And neon lights as bright as the sun close up
The sun has been cut from its birthplace
And enforced at the bottom of the best sculptured car *ever*
As I walk to school
I see the reflection of that once rainbow-coloured neon light
Shattered into a thousand pieces
That once blurry car
Was getting scraped off the dark, black pavement
The car that had stayed in the back of my mind
Then in my head I saw a different teenager getting in the car
And then speeding off
Suddenly I heard a *big bang*
And got thrown back
That once greatest Subaru *was no more.*

Ryan Dempsey (11)
Beck Primary School, Sheffield

The Beach

As I walked onto the beach today,
I picked up big pebbles on the way.
My dog had a wee right up a tree,
After that I took him and my sister in the sea.
We got a bit wet
To say that we had a bet.
Then we sat down and dried ourselves off.
We got some food from the takeaway called 'Scoff'.
Our mum came and we went home.
On the way we got an ice cream cone.

Billie Jo Holden (11)
Beck Primary School, Sheffield

What Is Pink?

(Based on 'What Is Pink?' by Christina Rosetti)

What is yellow?
A sun is yellow
Shining in the sky.

What is green?
Grass is green
Blowing on the earth.

What is blue?
A car is blue
Speeding on the road.

What is white?
A Polo is white
Refreshing the mouth.

What is violet?
A cloud is violet
Fluffing in the dark.

Reece James (8)
Beck Primary School, Sheffield

Bonfire, Bonfire

Bonfire, bonfire lights
Up so pretty. Sparks
Sprinkle away in the
Midnight sky.
As they
Move one by one they
Dissolve so slowly as
You watch them flow
Nicely then one more
Sparkles as it's flowing
Away.

Faye Mayfield (10)
Beck Primary School, Sheffield

What Is Pink?

(Based on 'What is Pink?' by Christina Rosetti)

What is pink?
A flamingo's pink standing while it blinks.
What is red?
Gryffindor is red showing off their bright robes.
What is blue?
A Cornish pixie of course
Pulling Neville Longobttom's ears up to the top of the ceiling
Saying, 'Why is it always me?'
What is white?
Nearly Headless Nick going, 'How do you do?'
What is yellow?
Hufflepuff is yellow showing off that bright badge.
What is green?
Slytherin is showing off that snake.
What is violet?
The clouds are floating around the world.
What is orange?
An orange is just orange.

Ryan J Wigley (9)
Beck Primary School, Sheffield

Days

Sunny days, cloudy days,
Days that are foggy
Days are like feelings on how they react
Most of us spend our days sitting in the house
Going on a bicycle for a ride
Playing is all we want to do
Laugh and play the days away.

Shantelle Clayton (11)
Beck Primary School, Sheffield

What Is Pink?

(Based on 'What is Pink?' by Christina Rosetti)

What is pink?
A rose is pink blowing in the mud.

What is yellow?
A sun is yellow shining in the fresh air.

What is white?
Clouds are white floating in the sky.

What is orange?
A fire is orange flaming in the garden.

What is blue?
The sea is blue flowing at the beach.

What is red?
A poppy is red standing still in the field.

Kelsey Hallam (7)
Beck Primary School, Sheffield

Bonfire Night

Fireworks shooting in the air.
Buds are splitting and it looks like petals are coming.
Your eyes are like fire on the ground.
Catherine wheels are like a shooting star.
Fireworks go as high as a bird.
Fires light up like autumn colours.
Bonfires burn like flowers popping.
Catherine wheels swirl like the wheels on a car.
Fireworks bang like thunder and crackle like lightning.
Toffee apples are as sticky as a stigma.
Sparklers sparkle like the sun is shining.

Alex Westney (7)
Beck Primary School, Sheffield

What Is Pink?

(Based on 'What is Pink?' by Christina Rosetti)

What is pink?
A poodle is pink swirling its big, round tail.
What is red?
Gryffindor is red being brave and smart.
What is blue?
Ravenclaw is blue like a blue balloon over the sea.
What is white?
Santa's beard's white just like the snow at night.
What is yellow?
Hufflepuff is yellow just like the sun at day.
What is green?
Slytherin is green following Snape's teaching.
What is violet?
The fat friar's violet flying over stars.
What is orange?
Well, just an orange.

James A Waddingham (8)
Beck Primary School, Sheffield

Untitled

The starlight from the sky,
The music when I die.
I go up to Heaven from Earth,
I lay there in peace, on my body is a mark of birth.
Hopefully I will be remembered,
I'll make your life one to remember.
You'll have had a successful life,
And you'd wish from the day you were born
You had me as your guardian angel.

Jodie Randall (10)
Beck Primary School, Sheffield

What Is Pink?

(Based on 'What is Pink?' by Christina Rosetti)

What is pink?
A pig is pink
While it's rolling in mud it makes a stink.

What is red?
A petal is red
When it falls off it lands on a soil bed.

What is blue?
The sea is blue
With a flashing shark passing through.

What is white?
The clouds are white
With a flying seagull passing by.

What is yellow?
The sand is yellow
While the sun shines in the sky.

What is green?
A greenfly is green
While it's flying it looks like a mean bean.

What is violet?
The fish are violet
As they dance to the stars.

What is orange?
The cats are orange
While they sing to the night stars.

Jake Evison (9)
Beck Primary School, Sheffield

What Is Pink?

(Based on 'What is Pink?' by Christina Rosetti)

What is violet?
Clouds are violet shining in the sky.

What is orange?
Fires are orange, bright in the garden.

What is red?
Roses are red, light and on the ground.

What is blue?
Sea is blue, flashing in the sea.

What is yellow?
A flower is yellow, glittery in a field.

Lauren Bradley (7)
Beck Primary School, Sheffield

High-Powered Rockets

Countdown commences . . . 3, 2, 1, *blast*
High-powered rocket flying so fast

Zooming past clouds, satellites, stars
Moving quickly on towards Mars

Heading back to Earth's home station
Computers full of space information

Men and women get out of the rocket
They plug their cameras into a socket

Seeing pictures they captured in space
Watching them all with a smile on their face

Look to the future not at the past
High-powered rocket flying so fast.

Oliver Flint (10)
Beck Primary School, Sheffield

What Is Pink?

(Based on 'What is Pink?' by Christina Rosetti)

What is pink?
A poodle is pink lying by the steamy cooker
What is red?
A sparkly pencil is red sitting in its pencil case bed
What is blue?
A balloon is blue floating up to the sky so high
What is white?
Snow is white that people make snowmen with
What is yellow?
A banana is yellow asleep in its fruit bowl bed
What is green?
Grass is green that covers up the muck
What is violet?
Wrapping paper is violet, it hides presents
What is orange?
A juicy orange is orange.

Bethany Hudson (8)
Beck Primary School, Sheffield

The World

The rivers flow
The winds blow
The cat jumped in a hat
The cat caught a rat
The children are singing
The church bells are ringing
Children gone to school
Grown-ups jump in the pool
Children writing
Babies biting.

Brandon Filler (10)
Beck Primary School, Sheffield

What Is Pink?

(Based on 'What is Pink?' by Christina Rosetti)

What is pink?
A cake is pink, very tasty I think!

What is red?
Ketchup is red when we spread it on our bread.

What is blue?
The sea is blue with dolphins jumping through!

What is white?
Snow is white, dazzling bright.

What is yellow?
Custard is yellow like swirling hot soup.

What is green?
Grass is green with clover blowing in the breeze.

Bradley Wilson (8)
Beck Primary School, Sheffield

What Is Pink?

(Based on 'What is Pink?' by Christina Rosetti)

What is pink?
A flower is pink swaying on the mud.

What is creamy?
A Labrador is creamy guiding people through the street.

What is green?
The grass is green waving on the ground.

What is white?
String is white swinging with a cat.

What is blue?
The sky is blue moving in the heavens.

Abigail Carlton (7)
Beck Primary School, Sheffield

What Is Pink?

(Based on 'What is Pink?' by Christina Rosetti)

What is pink?
A petal is pink, why bees come and look.

What is red?
A strawberry is red with pips stuck in your teeth.

What is blue?
A map can be blue, I need another clue.

What is white?
Paper is white, it's blank, clean and sharp.

What is yellow?
A pencil is yellow with me writing away.

What is green?
A meadow is green, all sparkly and clean.

What is violet?
A pot is violet, all bumpy and ragged.

What is orange?
A fire is orange with ashes burning between.

Leighton Ellison (8)
Beck Primary School, Sheffield

What Is Pink?

(Based on 'What is Pink?' by Christina Rosetti)

What is pink?
A cherry blossom is pink bursting in the bush.

What is red?
A fly-catcher plant is red catching flies in the woods.

What is green?
A crocodile is green hunting in the lake.

Charlotte Hearnshaw (8)
Beck Primary School, Sheffield

What Is Pink?

(Based on 'What is Pink?' by Christina Rosetti)

What is pink?
A dress is pink dancing in the sun.

What is red?
A bag is red hanging from the bed.

What is blue?
A ball is blue flying in the air.

What is white?
A car is white zooming down the road.

What is yellow?
The sun is yellow shining on me.

What is green?
The grass is green swishing side to side in the breezes.

What is violet?
A hat is violet blowing in the wind.

What is orange?
The sunset is orange going down on me.

Shannon Ledwood (9)
Beck Primary School, Sheffield

What Is Red?

What is red?
A fire is red burning on a garden.

What is green?
Grass is green with flowers in between on the ground.

What is black?
A bird is black flying in the sky.

Shaun Johnson (8)
Beck Primary School, Sheffield

What Is Pink?

(Based on 'What is Pink?' by Christina Rosetti)

What is pink?
A pig is pink while he rolls in the mud and blinks.

What is red?
A strawberry is red when it rolls to its soil bed.

What is blue?
A piece of Blu-tack is blue when it starts to stick like glue.

What is white?
Ice is white when it freezes in the night.

What is yellow?
The sun is yellow when it shines up in the bright light.

What is green?
The grass is green when it grows with lovely flowers in between.

What is violet?
The clouds are violet in the pretty night sky.

What is orange?
Why, just a plain, old orange in the shop for sale.

Samantha Machen (8)
Beck Primary School, Sheffield

What Is Silver?

What is silver?
A kettle is silver boiling in the kitchen.

What is blue?
A jumper is blue falling off the bed.

What is red?
A clock is red ticking on the wall.

What is white?
A straw is white sucking water from a cup.

Abby Turner (7)
Beck Primary School, Sheffield

What Is Pink?

(Based on 'What is Pink?' by Christina Rosetti)

What is pink?
A pig is pink rolling in the mud with a blink.

What is red?
A rose is red standing there with petals on its head.

What is blue?
The sky is blue where the clouds push through.

What is white?
A sheep is white in its nice warm coat.

What is green?
A grasshopper is green with its hopping legs.

What is yellow?
Paint is yellow drying on the wall.

What is violet?
Clouds are violet zooming through the night sky.

What is orange?
Just an orange.

Mitchell Cox (8)
Beck Primary School, Sheffield

What Is Pink?

(Based on 'What is Pink?' by Christina Rosetti)

What is red?
A flower is red, it is bursting out in the ground.

What is yellow?
A sun is yellow sparkling in the sky.

What is pink?
Blossom is pink growing on the tree.

What is green?
Grass is green waving in the ground.

Ellen Lee (7)
Beck Primary School, Sheffield

What Is Pink?

(Based on 'What is Pink?' by Christina Rosetti)

What is pink?
A flamingo is pink by the river having a drink.
What is red?
A tomato is red while it sits in its cold refrigerator bed.
What is blue?
The sea is blue with an octopus swimming through.
What is white?
The snow is white coming from the sky so high.
What is yellow?
Paint is yellow slooping on the walls.
What is green?
A car is green zooming on the road.
What is violet?
A bobble is violet on someone's hair.
What is orange?
Just an orange.

Nathaniel Buckle (8)
Beck Primary School, Sheffield

What Is Green?

What is green?
Grass is green growing in the ground.
What is gold?
A fish is gold sparkling in the sea.
What is white?
Glue is white, sticky on the table.
What is black?
A gate is black swinging on the ground.
What is blue?
Sky is blue shining in the sky.

Lauren Allen (7)
Beck Primary School, Sheffield

What Is Pink?

(Based on 'What is Pink?' by Christina Rosetti)

What is pink?
A pig is pink as it stands and drinks.

What is red?
A handbag is red as it swings in your mum's arms.

What is blue?
The sea is blue as the sharks swim through.

What is white?
A cloud is white as it floats through the light.

What is yellow?
Melons are yellow, fat, juicy and mellow.

What is green?
Leaves are green as they fall from the trees.

What is violet?
A plum is violet and cheers you up when you're feeling glum.

What is orange?
A balloon is orange and if you approach with a needle it will go . . .
Bang!

Conner Ramsay (8)
Beck Primary School, Sheffield

Bonfire Night

A rocket grows like a tree growing.
A Catherine wheel looks like a flower.
A toffee apple is as sticky as chewing gum.
A bomb rocket looks like a tree trunk when it opens up.
You can write your name with a sparkler beautifully.

Charlie Whiteley (7)
Beck Primary School, Sheffield

What Is Pink?

(Based on 'What is Pink?' by Christina Rosetti)

What is pink?
A pen is pink with me writing with it.
What is red?
A marble is red rolling around on the floor.
What is blue?
The sky is blue with clouds flying by.
What is white?
A piece of paper is white to draw, write and colour on.
What is yellow?
The sun is yellow burning as bright as can be.
What is green?
A Beck point is green to collect and exchange.
What is violet?
A colour is violet, a nice, bright colour.
What is orange?
An orange is orange, just a plain orange.

Alex Walker (8)
Beck Primary School, Sheffield

What Is Golden?

What is golden?
A fish is golden swimming in the pond.
What is green?
A pear is green eaten at home.
What is brown?
A kangaroo is brown jumping in the deserts of Africa.
What is blue?
A whale is blue swimming in the deep blue seas.
What is orange?
The sun is orange shining in the sky.
What is yellow?
A flower is yellow in-between the grass.

Kieran McKenna (7)
Beck Primary School, Sheffield

What Is Pink?

(Based on 'What is Pink?' by Christina Rosetti)

What is pink?
A pig is pink rolling in the mud while it sinks.

What is red?
An apple is red while it falls from a tree and bounces on your head.

What is blue?
The sea is blue rolling up and down as it goes.

What is white?
A seagull is white flying in the sky looking for some food.

What is yellow?
A crown is yellow on a queen or king's head to be royalty.

What is green?
Grass is green with flowers growing in the ground.

What is violet?
Violets are violet growing in the grass, growing fast.

Kerri Walker (8)
Beck Primary School, Sheffield

What Is Brown?

What is brown?
A bear is brown walking into the forest.
What is blue?
A wave is blue crashing against the beach.
What is red?
A boat is red sailing on the sea.
What is pink?
A pig is pink rolling in a mud farm.
What is green?
A monster is green crushing a town.
What is white?
Snow is white sprinkling in the sky.

Mackenzie Clarke (8)
Beck Primary School, Sheffield

What Is Pink?

(Based on 'What is Pink?' by Christina Rosetti)

What is pink?
A heart is pink beeping mentally

What is red?
An apple is red or it might as well be mouldy and dead

What is blue?
Blu-tack is blue, soft, roly and sticky like glue

What is white?
A computer is white, very clever, full of brains

What is yellow?
A lemon is yellow, very sour and pimply

What is green?
A greenfly is green going under people's ears

What is violet?
A grape is violet, sweet, juicy and round

What is orange?
An orange is orange, just an orange.

Callum Hudson (8)
Beck Primary School, Sheffield

Bonfire Night

Sparklers are like a bright star in the sky.
You can write your name like a bright light in the sky.
You can have a toffee apple that tastes like a lump of chocolate.
Rockets are like opening flowers spinning in the sky.
Bonfire Night is the best time of the year, you can see good stuff.

David Burnham (7)
Beck Primary School, Sheffield

What Is Pink?

(Based on 'What is Pink?' by Christina Rosetti)

What is pink?
A flamingo is pink while it's having a drink.

What is red?
Blood is red while it's pushing out someone's head.

What is blue?
The sky is blue while the clouds float through.

What is white?
Snow is white while it sparkles in the light.

What is yellow?
The sun is yellow, the sun is warm and mellow.

What is green?
The grass is green while it sparkles by the stream.

What is violet?
Grapes are violet hanging from a tree.

What is orange?
An apricot is orange while it's getting squished just like an orange.

Nicolle McCarthy (9)
Beck Primary School, Sheffield

Bonfire Night

Catherine wheels are like tyres on a car.
Sparklers are like a sparkling pencil.
The fireworks bang like the thunder and crackle like lightning.
Toffee apples are as sticky as glue.
The sausages sizzle like a fire.

Katie Flanagan (8)
Beck Primary School, Sheffield

What Is Pink?

(Based on 'What is Pink?' by Christina Rosetti)

What is pink?
A bag is pink while the perfume stinks.

What is red?
A hat is red as it sits on your head.

What is blue?
The sea is blue while the air blows it through.

What is white?
A computer mouse is white and all of a sudden it comes alive.

What is yellow?
Custard is yellow swirling with apple pie.

What is green?
Vegetables are green like a big broad bean.

What is violet?
A grape is violet, sweet, juicy and round.

Bailey Tickhill (9)
Beck Primary School, Sheffield

What Is Silver?

What is silver?
A fish is silver swimming in the water.
What is green?
Leaves are green blowing in the forest.
What is brown?
A kangaroo is brown hopping in Africa.
What is blue?
Waves are blue crashing on the beach.
What is red?
A boat is red sailing in the sea.
What is white?
Snow is white sprinkling in the sky.

Laura Embley (7)
Beck Primary School, Sheffield

What Is Pink?

(Based on 'What is Pink?' by Christina Rosetti)

What is pink?
A pig is pink and in the mud it can sink.

What is red?
A rose is red as it goes to doze in its soil bed.

What is blue?
A ball is blue coming off my shoe.

What is white?
The moon is white sparkling into the dark sky at night.

What is yellow?
A banana is yellow, nice and ripe and mellow.

What is green?
Grapes are green and they are getting crushed
And that is not a very good scene.

What is violet?
Candyfloss is violet in the night's twilight.

What is orange?
The sun is orange and it's just like an orange.

Sally Hampshire (9)
Beck Primary School, Sheffield

Bonfire Similes

A Catherine wheel looks like a spinning top.
A sparkler looks like a firework.
A firework is like a light bulb.
A rocket is as fast as a quad.

Kane Taylor (7)
Beck Primary School, Sheffield

What Is Pink?

(Based on 'What is Pink?' by Christina Rosetti)

What is pink?
A fox is pink while it slinks.

What is red?
A heart is red while it cares.

What is blue?
A bird's blue while it floats in the air.

What is white?
Paper's white while it rattles in the wind.

What is yellow?
A daisy is yellow while it says to the sun, 'Hello.'

What is green?
A grasshopper's green while it leans.

What is violet?
A book is violet while it sits and sleeps.

What is orange?
An orange is orange while it sits in your tummy.

Alex Brown (8)
Beck Primary School, Sheffield

Bonfire Similes

Fireworks shoot up like a shooting star.
Catherine wheels whirling round like a wheel on a bike.
A bonfire smells like a nasty plate of coleslaw.

Anees Botham (7)
Beck Primary School, Sheffield

What Is Pink?

(Based on 'What is Pink?' by Christina Rosetti)

What is pink?
A pig is pink rolling in the mud while it sinks.

What is red?
A rose is red waving in the breeze.

What is blue?
A ball is blue rolling off your shoe.

What is white?
A sheep is white chewing on grass at night.

What is yellow?
The sun is yellow brightening up the day.

What is green?
Grapes are green blowing off a tree.

What is violet?
Flowers are violet blowing in the wind.

What is orange?
A sunset is orange going down at night.

Liam Hoyland (8)
Beck Primary School, Sheffield

Stephanie

S tephanie is nice!
T igers are my favourite animal.
E njoy swimming.
P lay with my friends.
H ate pineapple!
A lways happy!
N ever nasty.
I love ice cream!
E ats a lot.

Stephanie Thomson (8)
Bonaly Primary School, Edinburgh

My Name Is . . .

My real name is Holly
But when I'm on my own,
I dream up names for how I feel,
Most of them quite unknown.

When I'm hungry, my name is Hungry Tummy,
Or sometimes Greedy Guts
Or Skinny Winnie.

When I'm angry, my name is Grumpy Mumpy,
Or sometimes Red Face
Or Moany Groany.

When I'm dreaming, I can do anything,
My name is Super Girl
Or sometimes Incredible Holly.

When I'm excited, my name is Crazy Girl,
Or sometimes Hyper Holly
Or Jumping Jack.

My real name is Holly
But when I'm on my own,
I dream up names for how I feel,
Most of them quite unknown.

Holly Passmore (8)
Bonaly Primary School, Edinburgh

Hannah

H annah is polite and kind.
A good girl.
N one of my friends are called Hannah the banana.
N ot very good at tidying.
A good worker.
H annah is my name.

Hannah Nicholson (8)
Bonaly Primary School, Edinburgh

Evacuee On The Train

I'm on the train.
I have never been in one.
I feel very scared.
Nobody is having any fun.

I am very bored.
There is nothing for us to play.
I can only talk to my friends
But there's nothing for us to say.

I cannot wait any longer.
I just stare down at the floor.
Why did this start?
Who started the outbreak of war?
They say it'll be over quickly.
I really hope that it will.
I hope none of my family get hurt
Especially my father who's ill.

I think we're nearly there.
We will arrive in Fife.
My mother sent me here
To save my precious life.

Kenneth Wong (11)
Bonaly Primary School, Edinburgh

These Hands . . .

These hands touch the nature all around.
These hands have cared for a baby tortoise of six months.
These hands have moulded a yellow clay frog with a pink tongue.
These hands have stroked Fizz and Smudge, my cats.
These hands drew the rainforest well.

Emma Black (9)
Bonaly Primary School, Edinburgh

The Dragons Inside Me

There is a curious dragon inside me
That makes me want to know lots of different stories
Which happen around my world.

There is a Tamagotchi-like dragon inside me
That makes me go to buy lots more!

There is a smart dragon inside me
That makes me work hard in school.

There is an artistic dragon inside me
That makes me want to draw lots of pictures at home.

There is a fun dragon inside me
That wants to get out and do something fun during school.

There is a sensible dragon inside me
That looks out when I'm crossing roads.

There is a sleepy dragon inside me
That makes me want to go to sleep really early!

Emma Bridges (9)
Bonaly Primary School, Edinburgh

These Hands . . .

These hands have played a full set of bagpipes.
These hands have touched a grey Aston Martin DB9.
These hands have made a black and green snake from clay.
These hands have slapped my brother on the face
When he annoyed me.
These hands have gripped golf clubs at St Andrews.
These hands have stroked an eagle at a centre for birds of prey.
These hands have played, touched, made, slapped,
Gripped and stroked.

Ross Newell (9)
Bonaly Primary School, Edinburgh

Leaving Home

I'm sitting on a train
Feeling lonely and sad
It has been a dull day
And I miss my mum and dad

I'm staring out the window
Watching the swaying trees
I can hear the wind blowing
I hope I stay safe please, please, please

I'm listening to the train's whistle
Blowing on and on
My parents can't forget me
Although I'm far and gone

I'm smelling a burning bonfire
I see the smoke rise up high
I imagine I'm sitting by a fire
I long for this to be a lie

I'm hearing the silence around me
I feel the soft hair on my doll
'I miss you so much, Isabell,'
I hear my parents call

I'm singing to make myself happy
And I am not alone
I think the whole train is now singing
But I still wish I was home.

Hilary Wood (11)
Bonaly Primary School, Edinburgh

Man U Debut

There once was a player from Man U
Who scored a goal on his debut
The player ran fast
And shouted, 'At last!'
But the goalie, he needed a tissue.

Robin Sloan (10)
Bonaly Primary School, Edinburgh

Evacuees

I'm sitting in the village hall
Thinking of my home
I turn round and realise
My brother and I are alone
I'm getting very worried
Because we're the last ones here
I look into my brother's eyes
And I can see the fear
I'm feeling very sick
My stomach is turning round
I smile at the billet officer
But she gives me a nasty frown
I'm looking at the clock
We're still in the village hall
Until the door opens
And in walks someone tall
I'm looking at the tall lady
Who walked in the room
The billet officer is looking at us
I know we'll be gone soon
I'm so happy, the tall lady picked us
We go and fetch our bags
She takes us home
Hand in hand.

Dania Eneser (11)
Bonaly Primary School, Edinburgh

These Hands . . .

These hands have created the winning poster in a competition.
These hands have stroked a thornback ray at Marine World.
These hands have felt chain mail that knights used to wear.
These hands have pointed to swimming penguins at the zoo.
These hands have applauded England's cricketers in the Ashes series.
These hands have thrown snowballs at my brother in winter.

Angus Hart (9)
Bonaly Primary School, Edinburgh

At The Station

Waiting at the platform,
Watching trains come in,
I am leaving from my London,
Will we ever win?

Here comes my train now,
Its steam is puffing high,
I do not want to leave London,
I do not want to say goodbye.

I am boarding the train now,
As well as many others,
Some are poking out their heads,
Saying goodbye to their mothers.

The whistle blows,
The steam is blowing,
The wheels are moving loudly,
The front of the train is turning.

I can smell the smoke now,
I can see my mum,
The train is loudly chugging,
And there I see the morning sun.

The train is round the platform,
I'm sitting with my friends,
I really, really, really do
Hope that this all ends.

Alasdair Grant (11)
Bonaly Primary School, Edinburgh

The Big Bee

There once was a young boy called Lee
Who one day went to the sea
When his mum was away
He got an ice cream without pay
And then got chased by a big bee.

Katie Wheelaghan (9)
Bonaly Primary School, Edinburgh

The Child Inside Me

There is a happy child inside me
That makes me smile and never frown.

There is an energetic child inside me
That makes me do cartwheels and run around.

There is a creative child inside me
That makes me paint really, really well.

There is a clever child inside me
That makes me do my maths extra swell.

There is a funny child inside me
That makes all my friends laugh.

There is a daring child inside me
That makes me climb mountains with big rocks.

These are the children inside me.

Anna Hazelwood (8)
Bonaly Primary School, Edinburgh

The Terrible War

Poppies rise from the ground
Where they have been disturbed
Soldiers lay fallen where they have been
Shot down dead
Gently wind picks up forming a slight whistle
Water far away forms into waves
Leaves cover the bodies like an
Immediate reaction
Smells of blood and gunpowder fill the air
Making a slight drowsy effect on the soldiers
Cannons boom out cannonballs
Making shrieks fill the air from frightened men
Being lost was terrible
Why did war have to come?

Natalie Matons (11)
Bonaly Primary School, Edinburgh

Apples

I was growing
Then there was a shake
I was falling down and down
From my tree
There was a thud, I was in a pot

I was taken to a big house
With giants everywhere
Before I could say ouch
I was in a hot room
Turning a funny colour

I was taken out
Chopped and sliced
I was apple pie!

Cara Pullar (8)
Bonaly Primary School, Edinburgh

Tomato Soup

I'm on a plant
All red and rich
I'm so warm I love it here
Then I'm in a basket
All itchy and cold
I'm in a pan being flattened
I don't like this
It is very painful, *ouch, ow!*
Next I'm in a pan
All hot and bubbly, all sweaty too
I'm put into a bowl
All creamy and salty
Then a spoon scoops me up
Now I'm tomato soup.

Anna Brown (8)
Bonaly Primary School, Edinburgh

Evacuees

I hear the whistle
As the train pulls away from the platform
I sit forward in my seat
Trying to see out of the window
I see my mum in the bustling crowd
She is waving at me
I wave back trying to hold back the tears
The train starts to pick up speed
I sit back in my chair
Hoping, wishing the war will soon end
The train starts to slow down
I hear the compartment door slide open
My teacher, Miss Brown, walks in
'Come on, get your things, we are here.'
I step onto the busy platform
Feeling scared and confused
The town hall is busy, bustling with people and scared children
I sit down and wait
Hoping that someone caring and nice
Will take me back to their home.

April Traynor (11)
Bonaly Primary School, Edinburgh

Food Poem

I am a potato
I live underground
One day someone picked me
I was mad
They took me to a place
Along with my dad
They made us into
Thin-cut chips
Already the children
Are licking their lips.

James Sturrock (8)
Bonaly Primary School, Edinburgh

Daddy's Gone Forever

What has happened to our family?
Why has it all gone wrong?
Daddy's gone forever
And Mummy's on her own

Everyone just seems so mad
My foster parents just sit and stare
Is it a crime to be sad?
Is this some kind of nightmare?

What has happened to our family?
Why has it all gone wrong?
Daddy's gone forever
And Mummy's on her own

My foster parents are so cruel
They run a ghastly farm
I just feel like a creaky tool
I don't mean any harm

What's happened to our family?
Why has it all gone wrong?
Daddy's gone forever
And Mummy's on her own

Our family is falling apart
My life is never-ending
All I'm now left with is a broken heart
And unfortunately it isn't mending.

Laura Cruickshank (11)
Bonaly Primary School, Edinburgh

Ida's Spider

There was a young girl called Ida,
Who swallowed a gigantic spider,
She shot into the sky,
And caught a huge fly,
Who's who? The spider or Ida?

Annie Forbes (10)
Bonaly Primary School, Edinburgh

Who Will Pick Me?

Who will pick me? Who will pick me?
Hardly anyone left now
Who will pick me? Who will pick me?
They all seem nice. Who will pick me?

Waiting, waiting. Who will pick me?
A good person or a bad person?
Sitting down, people pass. Who will pick me?
A lady passes with a glint in her eye.

Who will pick me? Who will pick me?
Hardly anyone left now
Who will pick me? Who will pick me?
They all seem nice. Who will pick me?

The lady passes again. 'I'll have him,' she says
I stand instantly, full of joy
'I'll be good.'
'You better be,' she replies.

Who will pick me? Who will pick me?
Hardly anyone left now
Who will pick me? Who will pick me?
They all seem nice. Who will pick me?

Bend down and pick up my case
Walk out the room and say to myself
This will be great
This will be great.

Who will pick me? Who will pick me?
Hardly anyone left now
Who will pick me? Who will pick me?
They all seem nice. Who will pick me?

Harris Penman (11)
Bonaly Primary School, Edinburgh

Oh Please

I can hear the rumble of the train's engine
I can feel the vibrations on the platform
I can see it charging its way over to where I stand
I can taste the fear on my fingers as I bite at my nails!

What can I do? What can I say?
Oh please, oh please, why can't I stay?

As I walk back I hold on to my mother
I never want to let go but I guess I'll have to!
Yes but I will have teddy, he will keep me safe,
Oh no, all alone in a carriage, I can't go!

What can I do? What can I say?
Oh please, oh please, why can't I stay?

I can hear the train screech to a halt
My heart skipped a beat, I feel such anger inside me
I want to run but my body is frozen
I just need to run, run, run, run!

What can I do? What can I say?
Oh please, oh please, why can't I stay?

So I run and I run but I soon fall
I am in such a state
Eventually Mother finds me
I cry and I cry so she says I can stay.

What can I do? What can I say?
I am just so glad that I can stay.

Annie Mackinnon (11)
Bonaly Primary School, Edinburgh

With Me Always

John and Peter,
They're gone but I remember them,
And as long as I remember, they're still here.

John, my friend whom I'll never forget,
Spread-eagled in front of me,
He is cold,
I'm reading a letter he'll never get to see,
In the letter John's sweetheart worries about his life in the trench,
Now she will worry no more.

Peter, my friend whom I'll never forget,
Staring at me from across the muddy wetness of the trench,
He is cold,
His arm lying limp over his chest,
The Bible clutched in his hand,
His hand covering his heart and many blood stains
Made by the bullets of the enemy's guns.

John and Peter,
Lain in front of me,
Under a mass of blood-red poppies,
They lie in peace,
A cross at their heads.

John and Peter,
They're gone but I remember them,
And as long as I remember, they're still here.
60 years ago I remembered them,
And I remember them still,
And because I still remember . . .
They will be *with me always.*

Bethany Frith (11)
Bonaly Primary School, Edinburgh

Alone

Will anyone pick me?
I feel so alone
Barely anyone's left
I just want to go home

The train is setting off again
I can see all the smoke
The smell is overwhelming
It's making me choke

Everyone's talking and walking
They're going away
To the home of the person
Fostering them today

Suddenly someone walks over to me
My eyes light up
But she's picked another evacuee
She gets up and walks away

I sit here for hours
A lonely evacuee
I think to myself
Will anyone ever pick me?

Someone comes over and looks at my tag
She scans it over with her big blue eyes
Suddenly she says, 'Come with me.'
I can't believe it, I think she's telling lies

I walk away
To my new home
I stare at the lady
And suddenly I don't feel alone.

Alison Robertson (11)
Bonaly Primary School, Edinburgh

Sitting In The Trenches

Sitting here, in the trenches
Corpses all around
Lying still, eyes wide open
Not making a sound

Sitting here, in the trenches
To be here is a curse
Digging and fighting
Nothing is worse

Sitting here, in the trenches
Russians and Brits lying together
Brutal fighting to the death
Soldiers gone to sleep forever

Sitting here, in the trenches
I don't want to die
Fighting for victory
I think I'm going to cry

Sitting here, in the trenches
We'll never taste defeat
I'm so tired
But I'll never take a seat

Sitting here, in the trenches
Writing a letter
Telling my family my last wishes
And hoping Dad gets better.

Tom Holligan (11)
Bonaly Primary School, Edinburgh

How It Feels

Waiting in the hospital with anticipation
Why is it always me in a situation?
While in the trenches, I couldn't be colder
A rotten German then shot me in the shoulder

When still in the trenches I got my mum's letter
Just reading it now, it makes me feel better
She is really quite funny, she put in some great lines
Like 'the house is quiet without you', or 'have a really great time'

The doctor comes in, my heart fills with dread
Then he tells me that I soon might be dead
I notice in that sentence that he had said 'might'
It doesn't necessarily mean that I will die tonight

The doctor also said 50% chance you'll live
All I can do now is try not to give
The Germans what they want, they want to see me dead
Shot by the bullet, not die in a bed

Back home in Scotland that's where I left my wife
I know that she would want me to fight for my life
If she came to see me I know she would start crying
Seeing me in the hospital, shot in the shoulder and dying

I'm going to give up on life, I'm in too much pain
It's all because of Adolf Hitler, that man's insane
I know I wouldn't live anyway, I know I would die
And up I go to Heaven and live with God in the sky.

Craig McMillan (12)
Bonaly Primary School, Edinburgh

The Experience Of My Life

I'm in the battlefield
I couldn't have more regrets
It's a misty day, I can hardly see
The bullets flying past me

The sound of the bagpipes is comforting
It makes me feel so happy
I can't wait to get home to my beloved mother
My sergeant shouts, 'Take cover!'

Suddenly they start to charge, the enemy is coming
I stand there still, sword in hand
This battle causes me such grief
However I must have belief

I feel a sudden urge to go and kill
My legs start to move
I run at the enemy, I can't stop
Suddenly I stop a man, sword in hand
I feel like I'm going to drop

I draw my sword and attempt to look brave
The man is no fool, I know this is the end
Then I hear the gunshot, the man crumbles to the ground
I was saved just by that one simple sound.

Oliver Eaton (11)
Bonaly Primary School, Edinburgh

The Last Run

Here I am, charging through mud and soil,
Why am I here?
To fight in the war, to make myself proud,
To crush my fear.

The yelling, the shouting is making me shiver,
I might fall to the ground.
I can hear my thoughts, nothing else,
Not the deafening sound.

The sky is musky, dark and brutal,
Making me shudder.
Troops of soldiers surround me now,
Charging and sweating, they fought.

Everything is turning into slow motion,
I'm starting to lose my breath.
I'm falling to the ground, I think I've been shot,
Is this going to be my death?

I'm losing my senses, I'm fading away,
I'm turning extremely dizzy.
Up, up I go, off to the heavens,
That was the last run.

Rachael Lynas (11)
Bonaly Primary School, Edinburgh

Poor Emma

Poor Emma doesn't understand
We're going to the countryside
Mother says it is safer there
We won't get hurt she tells us

Poor Emma doesn't understand
She keeps on saying she wants to take her bed
She says it will fit in her suitcase
Mother says it won't, as she checks my case

Poor Emma doesn't understand
She wants Mother to come with us
Mother said, 'Take your dolly,'
But I know we are going alone

Poor Emma doesn't understand
She presses her face against the window
Mother waves goodbye from the platform
But the train is moving and we are off to our new home.

Keri Millar (11)
Bonaly Primary School, Edinburgh

The Crane

There was a young boy from Spain
Who climbed to the top of a crane
Because he was dared
But got really scared
And never came down again.

Elizabeth King (10)
Bonaly Primary School, Edinburgh

Evacuees

As the sound of the wheels go
Round and round, round and round,
Round and round,
I think where I'll end up.
With a little old lady and a farmer man?
With an unhappy couple who'll be as strict as they can?
Round and round, round and round,
Round and round.
With a big, strong man who'll beat me up?
With a mother and father and a boy and his pup?
Round and round, round and round,
Round and around.
With a brother and sister with too many rules?
With a house full of children and a baby that drools?
Round and round, round and round,
Round and round.

Hannah Sneddon (11)
Bonaly Primary School, Edinburgh

Alliterative Animals

One wet walrus waggled his whiskers
Two terrible tigers twisted their tummies
Three thrilled thrushes thought about Thursday
Four feisty ferrets fought fiercely
Five female foxes felt the floor
Six stupid sloths sat on a slimy snake
Seven silly seagulls saw a seesaw
Eight enormous eagles ate an Easter egg
Nine nasty newts needed a nest
Ten tasty termites tore a token.

Duncan Porteous (9)
Bonaly Primary School, Edinburgh

The Train

I sit there tired, frightened, sad
Waving, crying
I might go mad

Chugga, chugga, chugga, chugga
The train is shaking

I spot Mother waving back
With Big Joe my brother
Carrying his gas mask sack

Chugga, chugga, chugga, chugga
The train is moving

I hear the engine come to life
I don't want to go
I'm only five

Chugga, chugga, chugga, chugga
The train is going

I see Mother running fast
But the train's too quick
And she stops at last

Chugga, chugga, chugga, chugga
The train is on its way.

Cara Rosie-Grice (11)
Bonaly Primary School, Edinburgh

Evacuee

The train is roaring down the track
Throwing me forward, throwing me back
Suddenly we come to a stop
The train has stopped and off I hop

Evacuee, evacuee
No one here to comfort me
Evacuee, evacuee
No one even looks at me

The only thing to do is wait
Why do I look such a state?
What will I do? Where will I go?
I just feel really low

Evacuee, evacuee
No one here to comfort me
Evacuee, evacuee
No one even looks at me

I'm all alone
And have no home
Sadness crawls over me
I want to be free!

Evacuee, evacuee
No one here to comfort me
Evacuee, evacuee
No one here to comfort me.

Julia Sergent (11)
Bonaly Primary School, Edinburgh

Untitled

Dear Mum, Lucy and darling Sally

I have been admitted to hospital with a broken leg.
Whilst I have been here thoughts of the battlefield
have been running through my head.
I have written them down in a poem for you.

Thinking of you by Private John Oakley

The Russian uniforms, brown in colour, march left, right, left, right
Lithe and quick just like little Lucy

Thinking of you

Sergeant James MacDonnell's huge sparkly badges
Glittering in the soft glow of the Russian autumnal moon
Remind me of Mum's face illuminated by the sun
Strands of hair covering the tell-tale wrinkles

Thinking of you

15-year-old William grinning, still grinning
Even though the gunfire rages all around him
Sally's face flashes to mind - eyes as bright as buttons

Thinking of you

The splint cutting into my leg is hurting
But the memory doesn't
Lucy cavorting round the kitchen
Feet encased in tiny ballet shoes

Still thinking of you.

Lena Reid (11)
Bonaly Primary School, Edinburgh

All Aboard

As we walk through the park
Through the shadows of the dark
Where are we going?
Shut your mouth
This is an awful task

'All aboard,' shouts the conductor
'Choo-choo,' shouts the train
We are going to the country
What a shame!

I don't know where we are going
I hope we won't be showing
My identity card
Or cleaning up the yard!

'All aboard,' shouts the conductor
'Choo-choo,' shouts the train
We are going to the country
What a shame!

When I was on the train
I got a really sore pain
As I waved goodbye to my mother
I set off with my wee brother

'All aboard,' shouts the conductor
'Choo-choo,' shouts the train
We are going away today
What a shame!

Ryan Ross (11)
Bonaly Primary School, Edinburgh

Before He Went

I went to pack my bag
So I put all my clothes in
When I was finished
I slipped my slippers in

I was very scared! I was very sad
When I went without my mum and dad

I clomped down the stairs
With my heavy suitcase
I popped it on the floor
Then I broke my mum's favourite vase

I was very scared! I was very sad
When I went without my mum and dad

I was so scared
I didn't eat anything
I was walking out the door to the bus
My mum said, 'Have you forgotten anything?'

I was very scared! I was very sad
When I went without my mum and dad

I gave my mum a kiss
And grabbed my stuff
I walked over to the bus and gave my mum a wave
On the bus I thought to myself, *I'll never forget my mum and dad*

I was very scared! I was very sad
When I went without my mum and dad.

Ryan Lynch (11)
Bonaly Primary School, Edinburgh

Why?

Why am I here?
I wish I hadn't volunteered,
I'm scared that I might die,
I'm scared of killing.
Why am I here?

Why the fighting?
Fighting never solved anything.
The guns and shells drive me crazy.
The aeroplane engines terrify me.
I hate the violence.
Why the fighting?

Why the trenches?
They are cold, cramped, wet and muddy.
Rats infest them and chew all our belongings.
Why can't we just live in tents?
Why the trenches?

Why the war?
What do the Germans want?
Why do they want to kill us?
I just want to go home to my family.
I want there to be peace.
Why the war?

Fiona Downie (10)
Bonaly Primary School, Edinburgh

Alone

Standing at the station
All alone
Waiting for the train
I don't know where I'm going
But there's no one to explain

All I see is faces
Tears trickling down their cheeks
They'll be going to different places
For weeks and weeks and weeks

Finally here's the train
Moving quickly through the gloom
But when I eventually get to the door
It turns out there's no more room

Once again I'm all alone
With no one to talk to and nothing to do
Wherever I go to stay
I might never see you.

Sam Peppiette (10)
Bonaly Primary School, Edinburgh

Apple Pie

I like to grow on trees
But I was picked up and put in a bag
With lots of different fruit
I was put in a box with apples
I felt all alone
I was picked up with clean, soft hands

I was sliced and boiled
Put in a pie, *crunch*, I was eaten.
Munch! Munch! Yum!

Megan B Hollis (8)
Bonaly Primary School, Edinburgh

Going Away

Choo-choo, choo-choo
Here comes the train choo-chooing along
'We're almost there,' shouts the driver
He rings his bell, *ding-dong*
Choo-choo, choo-choo

I can see the station away in the distance
I can smell the sheep in their fields
I can hear the trees swooshing in the wind
I can taste the Highland toffee strong in my mouth
I can touch the long grass out of the window

Choo-choo, choo-choo
Here comes the train choo-chooing along
'We're almost there,' shouts the driver
He rings his bell, *ding-dong*
Choo-choo, choo-choo

I can see some houses up in the hills
I can smell the smoke coming out the train top
I can hear the train chugging along
I can taste my lemonade stinging in my mouth.

Eliott Lockhart (11)
Bonaly Primary School, Edinburgh

Happiness

Happiness is like sunshine in the air,
It sounds like snow falling from the sky,
It tastes like strawberries lying in the fridge,
It smells like fresh air by a river,
It looks like children playing happily in the park,
It feels like a soft pillow lying on a bed,
It reminds me of the time
I went bowling with my mum on my birthday.

Irma Sadikovic (9)
Brockley Primary School, London

Love

Love is beautiful like when you feel something for someone,
It sounds like birds singing in your heart,
It tastes like softness in a hug,
It smells like roses in the air,
It looks like hearts flowing in the air,
It feels like the sea is making me happy in my heart,
It reminds me of my son and daughter in the future.

Kimberley Blackstock (9)
Brockley Primary School, London

Anger

Anger is horrid like a wolf ripping your soul,
It sounds like an evil laugh in my ears,
It tastes like eating stones for dinner,
It smells like death up my nose, down my veins,
It looks like terrible shadows in the dark chasing me,
It feels like a pumping heart in your hands,
It reminds me of nightmares making me shake in my bed.

Onur Ustaoglu (8)
Brockley Primary School, London

Love

Love is romantic like a boy kissing a girl,
It sounds like two hearts bumping together,
It tastes like ketchup, red like blood,
It looks like a heart beating,
It feels like my soul drifting away,
It smells like the flames from a bonfire.

Ben Hussein (8)
Brockley Primary School, London

Happiness

Happiness is the sun shining through the darkness,
It sounds like people playing in the park
Imagining that the sun will shine forever,
It tastes like spring sparkling through the light
And shivering through the dark,
It smells like the autumn trees waving their leaves,
It looks like the sun waving in the sky,
It feels like people sunbathing in the sky,
It reminds me of all the happy things I have done in my life.

Paige Bernard (8)
Brockley Primary School, London

Fun

Fun is wonder like happiness,
It sounds like children playing in the playground,
It tastes like some strawberries, fresh and sweet,
It smells like fresh air, cold and exciting,
It looks like kids playing 'It',
It feels like grass under your feet,
It reminds me of all of the good times in my life.

Kelly Louise Battle (8)
Brockley Primary School, London

Happiness

Love is beautiful like the spring sunflowers,
It sounds like a beautiful woman singing,
It tastes like butter with milk,
It smells like pretty flowers growing,
It looks like sunshine making things shiny,
Soft pillows on my bed,
It reminds me of when I open my Christmas presents.

Vanessa Vu (9)
Brockley Primary School, London

Anger

Anger is scary like a wolf ripping through your soul.
It sounds like a long-lost hyena in the darkness.
It tastes like frightening nightmares going through my mouth.
It smells like darkness and fear around me.
It looks like a zombie with its eyeballs popping out.
It feels like nightmares and fire from the devil in my brain.
It reminds me of darkness in the world.

Rommario McLeary-Campbell (8)
Brockley Primary School, London

Love

Love is the beauty like a lovely princess,
It sounds like the snuggling of two couples being married,
It tastes like love cake being cut by a couple,
It smells like the refreshment in a married couple's food,
It look like a lovely rose growing in the garden,
It feels like love spreading through the entire world,
It reminds me of my blanket, soft and lovely.

Titi Falade (8)
Brockley Primary School, London

Love

Love feels romantic like my heart will blow up
It sounds like singing in the breeze
It tastes like a rose, sweet and red
It looks like an angel flying around us
It feels like a breeze blowing calmly
It reminds me of my first date and kiss.

Tashauna Hall (9)
Brockley Primary School, London

Evil

Evil is like someone screaming just when they are going to be killed.
It sounds like someone evil laughing.
It tastes like sour green lemons.
It smells like decaying bodies.
It looks like someone dead on the floor.
It feels like the blood in my veins about to burst.
It reminds me of my great great grandad being killed in the war.

Max Biddle (8)
Brockley Primary School, London

Kindness

Kindness is gentle like smooth clouds.
It sounds like soft music.
It tastes like sour sweets.
It smells like the most wonderful melted chocolate.
It looks like shiny stars falling from Heaven.
It feels like stupendous, luxurious, fluffy pillows.
It reminds me of children being kind to each other.

Leanna Dixon (8)
Brockley Primary School, London

Evil

Evil sounds like a battle going on.
It tastes like blood dripping down my face.
It smells like a dead person lying on the ground.
It look like a ghost coming towards me.
It feels like a devil is laughing at me.
It reminds me of my mum shouting at me.

Rosharme Neubronner (8)
Brockley Primary School, London

Embarrassment

Embarrassment is empty like the colour white for zero.
It sounds like millions of people laughing at you
In a giant, black room.
It tastes like horrible, melting ice cream in a tornado.
It smells like bitter smoke from a fire going up your nose.
It looks like everyone looking at you and pointing with astonishment.
It feels like your life is nearly over.
It reminds me of walking into my classroom and wetting myself.

James Sirotkin (9)
Brockley Primary School, London

Laughter

Laughter is wonderful, a red rose waiting to smile
It sounds like a bass drum going through my ears
It tastes like lemon squirting on my tongue
It smells like perfume spraying around me
It looks like an orange waiting for me to take a bite
It feels like wind bellowing through my ears
It reminds me of my mum when I look around.

Dervell Rickman (8)
Brockley Primary School, London

Anger

Anger sounds like a man screaming in the street.
It tastes like bad, rotten eggs.
It smells like petrol.
It looks like blood on the floor.
It feels like people crying.
It reminds me of children crying for help.

Hasan Zafer (8)
Brockley Primary School, London

Anger

Anger is red like the blood of the Devil.
It sounds like drums in the deep.
It tastes like rotten tomatoes.
It smells like green elephant poo.
It looks like someone being shot in the heart.
It feels like fuzzy wasps.
It reminds me of terrorists.

Joel Levine (9)
Brockley Primary School, London

I Am Olivia

I can write a story over and over again
I can ride a pony around the universe in one minute
I know why blood is red
I know why cows say *moo!*
Why branches are bare in winter
I am Olivia
I know where stories come to life
Where the prickly porcupines hibernate
Where the flipcharts flip
Where buttercups go
I am Olivia
I know how many people use the computer a day
I know how many apples there are on one apple tree
How many stars there are in the sky
I know how many litres of water people use a day
I have been a stripy cat burglar
I have been a shooting star
I am Olivia.

Olivia Machell (8)
Colliers Green CE Primary School, Cranbrook

I Am Hannah

I can fly from sky to sky
I can run like the shooting stars
I am Hannah
I know why birds have colourful wings
I know why dolphins leap and dance at night
I am Hannah
I know where leaves fall in the summer
I know where clouds move during the day
I know where morning goes in the afternoon
I am Hannah
I know how many leaves there are on an old oak tree
I have been to a world of ideas
I have been a boulder on the Alps
I have been a rock in a pyramid
I am Hannah.

Hannah Moody (7)
Colliers Green CE Primary School, Cranbrook

I Am Rosie

I can run like sound,
I can fly like an eagle,
I know why snow is cold,
I know why my unicorn flies,
I know where dragons keep their fire,
I know how many stars there are in the sky,
I know how many stripes there are on a tiger,
I know how many raindrops fall from the sky each day,
I have been a pencil, a book, a shimmering knife,
I am Rosie.

Rosie Marsh-Rossney (7)
Colliers Green CE Primary School, Cranbrook

I Am Daisy

I can fly like a butterfly around the world in a second
I know why scientists are mad
I know why clowns are colourful
I know why shooting stars travel
I know why tears are a sign of sadness
I know where the land of pearls is
I know where the softest cloud is
I know where the smallest tree is
I know how many tears fall in a war
I know how many grains of sand there are in a desert
I know how many trees there are in a rainforest
I have been a swan
I have been a pig
I have been a snow leopard
I have been a tiger
I am Daisy.

Daisy Hutton (7)
Colliers Green CE Primary School, Cranbrook

I Am Emily

I can swim with a weight in my hand
I can drive a train
I know why the snow is white
Why the wind is invisible

I am Emily
I know where the rainbow ends
Where Saturn sleeps
Where stars are in the day
I know how many birds stay in the winter
How many tooth fairies there are
I have been to a secret galaxy
I have been a shivering horse
I am Emily.

Emily Lineham (7)
Colliers Green CE Primary School, Cranbrook

I Am Ellie

I can fly like a falcon
I can run like a lion
I can read Egyptian writing
I am Ellie

I know why lions are called lions
I know why dogs play in their dreams
I know why stars are sad and happy
I know where my fingers go at night
I know where dreams go in the day
I am Ellie

I know how many hairs are on a body
I know how many toes are in the world
I am Ellie

I have been a bit of dust
I have been a piece of hair

I am Ellie.

Ellie Deering (7)
Colliers Green CE Primary School, Cranbrook

I Am Verity

I can flutter along the deep, slippy ice
I can fly down a waterfall like a bird
I can tiptoe like a starfish in the sea
I can find the diamonds under the rocky soil
I can look at the swan all day in the sunshine
I know why zebras honk like a car
I know why sheeps' fur is like a cloud in the peaceful sky
I know why sunshine shines like a newborn baby's eye
I am Verity.

Verity Swallow (7)
Colliers Green CE Primary School, Cranbrook

I Am Lauren

I can make the littlest things turn to gold
I can fly swiftly around the world in a jiffy

I know why the frosted winter moon is so bright
I know why the tears of autumn trickle down your back

I know where the prickly porcupines hibernate
I know where the stories come to life
I know where the flipcharts flip

I know how many birds there are flying lightly across the skies
I know how many creatures are crawling around on the grass
This very minute

I have been a unicorn with a magical horn
I have been a woolly sheep, a cuddly bear

I am Lauren.

Lauren Swan (8)
Colliers Green CE Primary School, Cranbrook

I Am Lydia

I am the starlit night
I can climb a pyramid
I can shiver colder than the Arctic
I can swing with the monkeys through the rainforest
I know why there is a salty smell in the sea
I know why the sky moves by
I know why God is in Heaven
I know where space shuttles land
I know why clouds drop tears for rain
I know where the nose of the Sphinx is
I know where sky lands

I am Lydia.

Lydia Gerard (8)
Colliers Green CE Primary School, Cranbrook

I Am Mani

I can run like thunder
I know how many planets are in space
I know where the stars move
I know how many snowdrops are in one day
How many people like football
I know how many people like 'The Simpsons'.

Mani Coonjobeeharry (7)
Colliers Green CE Primary School, Cranbrook

Untitled

I am the rickerly river with twinkling fish.
I can see the future with ghosts.
I know the flames of a dragon.
I know where the moon rises up onto the sun
With stars twinkling upon it.

Ben Martin (8)
Colliers Green CE Primary School, Cranbrook

Chocolate Poem

Chocolates are good
Chocolates are bad
When they're all gone
You get very mad
Some are soft
Some are hard
When your mum eats them
You feel sad because she ate them
Then she buys you more
And then you feel glad.

Francesca Kate Shimmin (10)
Cottingley Village Primary School, Bingley

Chocolate!

Yum-yum, yum-yum!
Chocolates and sweets
I love them both
All runny and soft
They truly bring delight
Oh chocolate, oh chocolate
You melt in my mouth
Sometimes I wonder how
You were made
You make my mouth
Water sometimes like a
Dog. You make me faint
When I pop you in my mouth
It's like you say, 'Eat me, I'm
Really nutritious.' I know you are
Unhealthy but I just can't
Help myself!

Luke Foster (9)
Cottingley Village Primary School, Bingley

Christmas

It is Christmas, snowy and bright.
We put up the Christmas tree with shiny, bright lights.
Outside where the snow is laid
My mum said you could draw a snow maid.
My mum got the camera with a big shiny flash.
Then I said, 'I'm putting on my Christmas sash.'
It is Christmas, snowy and bright.
We put up the Christmas tree with shiny, bright lights.

Charlotte Hill (9)
Cottingley Village Primary School, Bingley

Weathers, Colours And Patterns

Thunder is when I'm angry
Sun is when I'm happy
Rain is when I'm crying
Cloudy is when I'm sleepy
Snowy is when I'm cold
Hail is when I'm cross.

Orange is when I'm excited
Green is when I'm ill
Blue is when I'm tired
Red is when I'm cross
Yellow is when I'm hungry
Black is when I'm bored.

Spotty is when I'm happy
Zigzag is when I'm excited
Plain is when I'm sad.

Jenny Bedford (9)
Cottingley Village Primary School, Bingley

Feeling Good

Feeling good, a very nice feeling.
Feeling good, something that you can always be.
Feeling good, it makes you happy
Because there's nothing better than feeling good.

Feeling good, a very nice feeling.
Feeling good, something you can always be.
Feeling good, it makes you happy
To feel happy you have to feel good.

Faisal Darr (9)
Cottingley Village Primary School, Bingley

Chocolate!

Chocolate is really yummy
It really fills me up
And amuses my tummy
Especially when it's melted

I love melted chocolate
It is really nice
'Cause you get lots of flavour
And the taste is very lovely

Oh you should really try some
So you know I'm not lying
I think you will agree with me
When you try some chocolate!

Oh you ought to try some
Please don't keep me waiting
Come, just reach into the fridge
And eat some *chocolate!*

Alex Howell (9)
Cottingley Village Primary School, Bingley

Winter

Slowly falling snow,
All white and soft.
People hang up decorations,
For the birth of Jesus.
People make a list for Santa,
For him to bring with Rudolph.
People make snowmen,
And snowballs and have fun.

Grace Lawson (10)
Cottingley Village Primary School, Bingley

Happy And Sad

When I am happy
I feel I am
Upon a unicorn.

But when I am
Sad I feel like
No one will play
With me.

When I am happy
I feel like I
Am in Chocolate
World.

But when my rabbit
Dies I will be
Very, very, very sad.

Juwayriyah Z Ali (9)
Cottingley Village Primary School, Bingley

The Meaning Of Chocolate

C reamy
H appy
O ozing
C aramely
O ooh!
L ovely
A luxury
T asty
E xtraordinary

and that's the meaning of chocolate!

Chloe Lupton (10)
Cottingley Village Primary School, Bingley

Being A Rainbow Dolphin

Being a rainbow dolphin
You'd be brighter than a dustbin
You could jump over the rainbow
Showing off all your colours, you'd be the star of the land

All your friends would look at you in amazement
Look at all your colours, you'd have a movie star tent
Then one day you'd look at yourself
And all your colours have gone.

You'd feel very upset
Because no one would notice you anymore
You'd try to jump
But you couldn't jump over the rainbow
Suddenly you awake, good, it was all a dream

You'd look at yourself,
You weren't really a rainbow dolphin
It was just all a dream.

Rafiah Khan (10)
Cottingley Village Primary School, Bingley

My Poem About War Combat

The bullets spit at the soldiers
Like a flurry of hailstones,
As the bullets hit the trench
The soldiers' spirits sink!

But although their spirits sink
They soar up like an eagle in flight;
The guns have stopped,
Stopped like the woodpecker stops to rest.
But, oh no, the bullets have started again,
They are like trains screaming into the station.
Sadly though the train cannot stop as the war goes forever on.

Martin McLaughlin (10)
Elworth Hall Primary School, Sandbach

Women At War

War girls are bricks; standing strong,
Some men are yelling in pain.
Running, blowing the air raid whistles,
Suddenly starting to rain.

Farmers farming, digging up crops,
War girls working hard.
Factory girls making ammunition
Fast as a speeding Spitfire.

Sirens screaming, shelters sighing,
Public wanting to cry.
As everyone walks; the planes attack,
All screaming, *'Get a life!'*

Whilst planes keep screaming overhead,
Nazis dropping bombs.
Sneakily Hitler runs away
Winston doesn't get a say.

Calum Elder (11)
Elworth Hall Primary School, Sandbach

Evacuation

Saying goodbye to Mum and Dad,
Looking very glum and sad,
People laughing, people crying,
Not knowing who is dying.

Every child not knowing where they are going,
Wondering if they will do any sewing,
Then the train comes to a stop,
And all the children run and hop.

Amy Kay (10)
Elworth Hall Primary School, Sandbach

War Times

Bombs drop fast as trains
Dropping up high from planes
War girls are bricks - standing strong
When they've done they sing a sad song

When the bombs drop
The sound's more than a pop
Little children asleep in bed
They wake hoping not to be dead

The sirens make a dreadful sound
Then sadly the bomb hits the ground
All the children feeling sad
All the Germans are very bad

The soldiers are bricks
Straight and brave
While war girls
Work hard all day.

Carrie Smith (10)
Elworth Hall Primary School, Sandbach

Spitfires In The Air

The Spitfires gliding in the air.
Gently floating down like a soft tissue,
Falling to the ground.
Whilst poppies are blooming field to field
Like nothing was happening.
Bombs constantly going off.
Bang! Bang!
I wish just in one word it would stop
But no!
Rationed petrol like sticky glue.
It's like this will never end!
The soldiers are stone and the women are rock.

Joshua Styles-Iddon (10)
Elworth Hall Primary School, Sandbach

Air Raids

Loud screeching wails
That the siren is making.
Scary and blaring, warning us wildly!
Hear the bang of a bomb landing angrily.
Hear the scream of the planes falling shamefully!

Hear the worried moan of the barrage balloons.
People shouting, 'We hate Hitler,' angrily.
Some shouting, 'We don't.'
Me saying, 'I hate this, why can't it stop?'

Climbing into the draughty bomb shelter, shivering.
Tears running down my face.
The world falling down all around us!
Unfixable!
Mum brings some mattresses and sheets for my bed!
I see it now, it's obvious! We're sleeping here instead.

I run like a fast train, I cannot stay in there!
The water smells like wet clay, the walls like mouldy bread.
The floor is flooded like a small pond.
I won't sleep in my own grave!

The all clear's here. My heart stops thumping.
I wipe away a tear then I run home.
Will my mum be there?
Alive or dead?
I panic! Home is strange, scary and quiet!
What will become of me?

Natalie Mason (10)
Elworth Hall Primary School, Sandbach

The War Girls Saved Our Lives

Before the war broke out,
Women were used as housewives.
But after that it all changed,
And war girls saved our lives.

When the men went to war,
Women were left behind,
Saying goodbye, not knowing what to do,
Left doing jobs of all kinds.

So step away from the sink, ladies,
Have a go at something worthwhile!
Build a house, knock down a wall,
And maybe stick up a tile!

Be the bricks, be the glue;
Hold this world together.
Show you've got some talent,
So try and work forever!

Be like a machine,
So fast, so furious and strong.
Don't stop, the machines will howl without you,
We've got to get along!

When the men come back,
You know they will push you out.
Don't let them, have some sturdiness,
You know they can't do without.

So now the war has ended,
And they've done just what I said;
Be like you were before
And you'll end up being fed!

Sophie Hindley (10)
Elworth Hall Primary School, Sandbach

War Girls

Whilst men made bullets scream into the night
Ladies didn't hesitate to fight
Working in factories everywhere
Making ammunition to send everywhere

When the sirens screeched out
Women stayed in the factories without a doubt
Working all day long
Whilst singing joyful songs

Whilst women worked all day long
Men fought shamefully
Looked in their minds for a loving memory
War girls were machines racing through their work.

Megan Standring (9)
Elworth Hall Primary School, Sandbach

Women At War

Whilst men are making bullets
That scream into the night,
Women shall work - not fight.
Working in factories or even on farms,
Ladies didn't hesitate to stay calm.

When sirens screeched out,
Women stayed at work without a doubt.
Working all day long,
Whilst singing a joyful song.

Women worked like brave soldiers,
As men fought to make Germans run home.
As the days are gone,
Ladies will be gone.

Hannah Elder (9)
Elworth Hall Primary School, Sandbach

Evacuees' Lives

Evacuation is so unfair,
Leaving home and not knowing
Where you're going.
Staying in the country,
It's all quite different to home.

The train runs along the rails
And it takes you a long, long way.
Evacuees are loaded on
And there is more on the trail.

They are lions
Enclosed in a zoo
And the train is a cage.
Whilst the bombs are falling on their homes
They are making a journey to safety.

Rebecca Withington (9)
Elworth Hall Primary School, Sandbach

Wartime

Air raids screeched all night long
While people screamed and ran away
Spitfires whizzed through the air
As people stopped to look and stare

Shelters were as tough as rocks
People hid from the bombs
Bombs dropped through the sky
Children looked and started to cry

Soldiers were statues, strong and proud
While war girls worked with not a sound.

Lydia Smith (10)
Elworth Hall Primary School, Sandbach

Back In 1939

Guns are spitting bullets left and right,
Whilst the people are in their shelters they might,
Hear the sirens scream like the wind.

Bang, bang, bang, bang!
Suddenly the sirens whisper then stop,
Quickly the people get out to see,
That another bomb has dropped.

In the next village trains go past,
Filled with evacuees to the brim,
Some are crying, some are pale,
Their lives look like they're extremely dim.

The war is over and a lot of people are dead,
But we have to look forward to our life ahead.

Becci Scott (10)
Elworth Hall Primary School, Sandbach

The War Girls

The war girls work all day long
When they work they whistle a song

The war girls' clothes, tatty and mangled
Their hair all tacky and tangled

War girls don't fight
Despite hearing bombs in the night

The bombs smack the ground
Loads of people shouting all around

Each war girl does her job
They never cry or sob

The war girls are tough bricks
They never turn around and get in a mix.

Emily Wright (9)
Elworth Hall Primary School, Sandbach

Bombs Fall

Bombs fall to the ground
When they fall they make a sound.

The bombs drop fiercely
Like thunder and lightning.

When the bombs hit the floor
They bounce around.
Then *bang, bang, bang!*

Bombs drop in the sky as fast as a moving train
Then hit the ground as hard as a heavy weight.

Bombs are launched from German planes
But the Germans can't really aim
They end up hitting their own spies.

Now the war is over
And soldiers are dead
We hope there's not a war ahead.

Aimee Bendall (10)
Elworth Hall Primary School, Sandbach

World War II

Flying the planes up above,
Hear it screaming when it passes,
Dropping as fast as trains,
As the guns spit bullets in the air.

War girls are bricks, standing strong,
When they are done they sing a happy song.
The windows shake when bombs drop.

In the city, at the station,
Trains are waiting.
Then the evacuees pile in.
Some are crying, some are sick,
Life is not very happy for them.

Shannon West (10)
Elworth Hall Primary School, Sandbach

War!

Soldiers stand straight and proud,
They are spirited like the other ones.
Standing still as still as a statue,
They fight and fight all day long.
They do it for a lot of years.
They starve and are thirsty.
They freeze and go blue
Then at night-time the guns spit.
Bang, bang, bang!
The air raid sirens really scare me,
They are as deafening as an exploded bomb.
I retreat to the shelters.
They stink and are dark and worst of all
Rats scurry around me.
My shelter is bars of iron
And when a bomb falls I get terrified.

Kate Highfield (10)
Elworth Hall Primary School, Sandbach

Fly High

I fly high in the war
I make myself win
The planes shoot bullets at me
I die from being murdered.

You think so much about their dreams
You'll never get to hear them
They risked their lives for everyone but themselves
We miss you
We miss you
But thank you.

Sarah Entwisle (9)
Elworth Hall Primary School, Sandbach

War Girls!

As the bullets bellowed into the night,
The women fought for what was right.
Some were sparrows, rushing to do their jobs,
While others were like cheetahs, working impossibly fast.
From the orange dusk to the blood-red dawn,
The ladies worked without so much as a yawn.
The machines screeched at being worked so hard,
But for everything made the men gained a yard.
Still some preferred home,
But their anxiety was crushed by other's humour.
One woman drove the van,
While others did what they can.
The war brought out the best in them,
With a bravery not to condemn.
The women worked tirelessly like bulls,
While some helped the ships, watching the hulls.
While some held on to their wedding rings,
But some on the farm used to sing,
'There isn't any use for delicate blouses,
When you're working with pigs and cowses.'

Simon Banks (10)
Elworth Hall Primary School, Sandbach

Britain's At War

The men fought valiantly in the Great, Great War
But once again the guns are fired.
Britain is at war without a doubt.
The Germans are back to try and beat us.
They're bombing our fields inconsiderately.
As the sirens scream the children run.
We must stop these monsters or we'll be stopped.
The war has nearly ended as the last guns are fired.
We mustn't give up hope for we all must do our part.

Daniel Ashcroft (11)
Elworth Hall Primary School, Sandbach

War Girls

War girls, underestimated power
Pulling the war but pulling no credit
Brave as men, tough as warriors
War girls were the tiny cats unnoticed
Working the factories on solitary nights
Lonely and reclusive they were
But duty-bound they carried on
They clattered the sirens
They stopped all the trains
They worked the nation
But no appreciation came
To these tireless souls
Who worked themselves dry
Just the knowledge they
Had done their jobs well
War girls we will remember
Nursing the wounded
Keeping the home, doing nothing but work
But still these lions withstood
Forever and more they did
And carried on
They had been watching and waiting
And listening for their moment but it never came
But they still worked, never stopped
Until it was all over
They never saw the glory
War girls we will remember.

Joseph Watts (10)
Elworth Hall Primary School, Sandbach

War Girls

Straining their muscles whilst working hard
As tough as new bricks standing tall
Even though war was all around them
They struggled on all alone

All through the night they do their jobs
Working until their eyes grow red
They hear the aircraft overhead
Stumbling through the sky

On the farmland where the cattle rest
A farmer: a girl, works her best
As strong as steel she carries on
Hoping that war will stop haunting her head

The nurse in a hospital
A soldier with wounds
Looking after the patients
Thinking of war

Then as the bullets' loud roars seize up
Women in factories leave for the night
Glad to be resting in bed for some time
But worrying about war that is not fine.

Rebecca Greenbank (9)
Elworth Hall Primary School, Sandbach

World War II

Whilst the sirens scream with fright
Men get ready to go and fight
Women run around looking after children

Then as the guns spit out the bullets
We all scream in fright,
'Get in the shelters, get in the shelters!'

Then the bombs drop and smash the sandbags
The bombs are thunder-loud and furious
We all shudder in fright like a train as it stops
Now it is all over we all come out
The wardens are made of steel as they come out first
In front of the bombs.

And now it is all over
We can clap and play
Even though people have died
We've still won and feel pride.

Zoë Hursthouse (10)
Elworth Hall Primary School, Sandbach

Landing Craft

Landing crafts are strong trolls
Coming swiftly like a swallow
Full with terrified men
Never stopping
Always coming
Bloodstains all over
The raft drops quick and steady
Men scream in pain
A pool of blood forms on the floor
Bits of brain sliding down the wall
What a terrible war
How did it occur
In these six years of blood and gore?

Alex Wilding (10)
Elworth Hall Primary School, Sandbach

Women's War

Women worked in factories everywhere
Doing a job they weren't trained for
Working day and night
Being able to help but not to fight
Women are machines racing through their work.

Women are sewing all they can
Helping as much as possible
Doing men's jobs
Just as well as men can
Even without a sob
Men are statues standing strong and proud.

Some women nurses go out to help
Taking care of wounded soldiers, trying to make them better
Women worked in factories - standing strong
Doing their job, nothing going wrong.

Alyssa Hargrove (10)
Elworth Hall Primary School, Sandbach

The Ghost Town

This is a ghost town in the Wild Wild West,
No one else lives here, not even a soul.
It's just me and my trusty gun.
There's something here, but I don't know what.

Many stories are told of that fateful day.
Some say I bumped into the Devil but I say nay.
Some bandits came, I chucked one down a well
But for the rest of them, I blasted them to Hell.

Joseph Wilkinson (10)
Hallaton CE Primary School, Market Harborough

Roby Smith

Roby Smith came from far away,
And he only went to school on a Monday,
He hadn't got one single friend.
He thought his misery would never end.
He bit his nails all dark and black,
His hair covered in dirt, his teeth covered in plaque.

Roby Smith has been adopted.
His parents died in a car crash, he wished he'd stopped it.
Roby Smith is beaten and battered,
His hair's in a mess, his clothes are all tattered.
So he sits there alone, every night,
Wishing his life would one day go right.

Thomas Bridgewater (11)
Hallaton CE Primary School, Market Harborough

Scary Mary

Scary Mary has dark blue toes,
Scary Mary lives in Black Bat Cove,
Scary Mary will eat your hair,
Try and touch her if you dare.

She'll feel your ears, she'll suck your fingers,
By your house is where she lingers.

Her snow-white feet, her icy eyes,
She sat in the corner and started to cry.
Many people were shocked with fright
When they saw her dead body in the night.

Erin Sanders (9)
Hallaton CE Primary School, Market Harborough

Billy Crescent

Billy Crescent sits alone,
Silently thinking of a place to call home.
A fishing rod in one hand, stale bread in the other.

An Irish wolfhound lies at his side,
His hand ruffles its shaggy hide.
He dreams of a hug from his long-dead mother.

Fergus Kennedy (10)
Hallaton CE Primary School, Market Harborough

Faded Love

I remember the cloud's whisper
I remember the sunshine,
I remember the love of him,
The love was all mine!
Our hands always touched,
I thought we'd be one forever,
But now you're gone,
You're gone forever, we're not together!
Do you remember me?
Will you ever see?
You're in my mind, you see,
I see you in my dreams.
I remember the day you felt ill,
Since then, it's not been the same.
I remember when you crashed your car,
The hospital rang, I thought I was to blame.
I said, 'Don't leave.'
You said, 'I will never leave you.'
You're still in my heart,
Your words still speak the truth.

Charlotte J Berisford (11)
Hallow CE Primary School, Worcester

My Life Is Over Now . . .

My life is over now,
There is no point in me living
If I saw you again, I would bow.

My life is done,
Why did you die?
There is no more fun,
You knew I'd never lie.

I wish you could come back,
I have tried my best,
I cry every night,
But it never works.

My life is over,
The sun doesn't shine,
The day we kissed stays in my mind.

The aroma of the red rose
Is always by my nose.
I visit you every day
But it doesn't change.

My life is over,
See you in Heaven, my love.

Bethany Rose Griffin (10)
Hallow CE Primary School, Worcester

I Love You

Roses are red, violets are blue
You are wonderful
I want to be with you
When you come outside the clouds disappear
All bad memories fade
I love you
I think of you every day
When I go to work.

Bradley James (10)
Hallow CE Primary School, Worcester

My Love Has Faded Away

You were as light as a feather
As beautiful as a star
And as clever as can be,
But now my love has faded away.

You were always jolly
With a sweet, sweet smile on your face
And every time I was unhappy
You always made me cheerful
But now my love has faded away.

Even though you left me
You are always in my heart
I think about you day and night
But now my love has faded away.

Bradley Bailey (11)
Hallow CE Primary School, Worcester

I Would Do Anything For You

If I wrote a book,
It would be about you.

Because I love you,
But I can't,
Because I'm not an author.

If I were king,
You would be my queen.

Because I love you,
But I can't,
Because I'm not that powerful.

Max Smith (10)
Hallow CE Primary School, Worcester

If I Were . . .

If I were a runner,
I would run for you,
If I were a baker,
I would bake you a cake,
But I am only an average man,
So I give you my love.

If I were a millionaire,
I would give you millions,
If I were a clown,
I would make you laugh,
But I am only an average man,
So I give you my love.

If I were an artist,
I would paint you a picture,
If I were a musician,
I would write you a love song,
But I am only an average man,
So I give you my love.

Oliver Reakes-Williams (10)
Hallow CE Primary School, Worcester

The Love That Never Died

If I were an artist I'd paint
A picture for you
If I were a sculptor I'd make you out of stone
Also if you were poor, I'd still love you.

If I were a musician I'd write you a song
If I were a gardener I'd plant you a bed of roses
If I were a superhero I'd save you from anything
If I were a carpenter I'd make you a wooden heart.

And I'd do that all for you.

Dan Pearson (10)
Hallow CE Primary School, Worcester

If I Were A . . .

If I were a poet,
I'd write poems for you.
If I were an artist,
Paintings too.
But as I'm just a boring man,
I give you my heart
As best I can.

If I were a sportsman,
I'd give you my gold.
If I could make them,
I'd give you my goals.
But as I'm just a lonely guy,
I need your love,
Or else I will cry.

Ben Tolhurst (10)
Hallow CE Primary School, Worcester

If I Were A . . .

If I were a singer
I'd sing for you.
If I were a marathon runner
I'd run for you
But as I'm just an average man
I give you my love
As best I can.

If I were a prince
You'd be my princess
If I were a musician
I'd play for you
But as I'm only an average man
I'll give you my love.

Alexander Shaw (11)
Hallow CE Primary School, Worcester

How Much I Love You

I would rather have you than the stars,
I love you more than the planet Mars,
You are more beautiful than the sun
And I love you.

You are better than a summer's day,
You are better to look at than the children at play,
You are brighter than a field of poppies
And I love you.

You're as clever as can be,
You are way more beautiful than me
And I love you.

You are happy and full of joy,
You are way better than my old best toy
And I love you.

David Harris (10)
Hallow CE Primary School, Worcester

Love Poem

The moon glows just like your eyes,
I wish I could fly,
Higher and higher in the sky.

You smell of lavender
Your aroma makes me faint
I would put up a fight just to be with you,
I would walk a mile to make you smile.

You make me feel brand new.

Lewis Bishop (10)
Hallow CE Primary School, Worcester

Butterfly

The time has come
For the butterflies to flutter,
To fly away from here
Together.

They fly gently,
They turn faintly,
Gliding through the sky,
Together.

The time has come
For the butterflies to flutter,
To fly away from here
Together.

Ashley Williams (10)
Hallow CE Primary School, Worcester

The Lover Died

The ship has sunk, my heart is broken,
Turn out the light,
At night,
I send you love,
I would work for you,
For love,
If I were a poet,
I would make a poem,
So if I were a gardener,
I would plant you a flower,
I will love you for anything,
Also, if I were a carpenter,
I would make you a chair,
I would dare.

Samuel Tillen (10)
Hallow CE Primary School, Worcester

Love Has Died

Our love has died,
Every day I have cried.

I have never felt so sad,
I feel so bad.

I really want you to come back,
I'd give you millions of gold in a sack.

Words won't bring you back because I've tried,
Tears won't bring you back because I've cried.

I love you, my dear, I will never forget,
The first time that we ever met.

I have dreams of you and me under the stars,
Looking through a telescope at Mars.

Eleanor Latham (10)
Hallow CE Primary School, Worcester

How Much I Love You

If I were a paper maker
I would make you a card
If I were a carpenter
I would make you a wooden heart
If I were an actor
I would write a play about you
If I were a gardener
I would get you a rose
If I were a shopkeeper
I would get you what you want
If I were a carpet maker
I would make you a tapestry
If I were an artist
I would make you a sculpture of your head.

James Nichols (10)
Hallow CE Primary School, Worcester

What I Would Do For You!

If I were a runner,
I would run you a marathon.
If I were a builder,
I'd build you a house.
If I were a footballer,
I'd score you a goal.
If I were a chef
I'd cook you a treat.
If I were a farmer,
I'd give you my best cow.

But I'm just a normal man
And I'll give you anything I can.

Alex E Stratford (10)
Hallow CE Primary School, Worcester

Put Out The Light

Put out the light,
Wash out the sea,
The mosquito bite,
Is not for me.

Sink the ship,
Blow the tree,
Paint the sky,
Just for me.

Light the sun,
Plant me a tree,
Destroy the gun
And graze the knee.

Is this a poem
Just for me?

Thomas Bratton (10)
Hallow CE Primary School, Worcester

If I Were A . . .

If I were a fortune teller,
I'd bet anything that you would be a super model.

If I were an archaeologist,
I'd save all the treasures for you.

If I were a carpenter,
I'd make lots of things for you.

If I were a shopkeeper,
I'd give you a special offer.

Oliver Holden (10)
Hallow CE Primary School, Worcester

Football - Haiku

Football is so fun
And the atmosphere is great,
The goals are the best!

Rahaab Sharif (11) & Lamar Stevens (10)
Heavers Farm Primary School, South Norwood

Ice Cream - Haiku

Soft, melting ice cream,
Lick it quickly, don't be slow,
Mine is chocolate.

Keighley Powell & Eden Hutchinson (11)
Heavers Farm Primary School, South Norwood

Dogs - Haiku

Hairy and smooth pets,
Loud and scruffy and so fast,
Sleeping on the job.

David McNamara (10)
Heavers Farm Primary School, South Norwood

Animals

I am an animal that lies in a tree
Can you guess what I could be?
I am as black as coal,
But I am as strong as an angel's soul.
'Listen down there you two,
I am hungry, so watch out, I might eat you.'

Have you guessed what I could be?
I will give you a clue,
If you come too close
I will pounce on you!

A panther.

I am a man's best friend,
I am an animal that you can depend,
I will fetch your papers in the morning,
When I hear you yawning.

Can you guess what I could be?
I am as busy as a bee,
I am for life, not just for Christmas,
You will want to get me 'cause . . .

I am well house-trained,
Because when I was little I got caned,
Have you guessed, I'm a dog,
Not a cat, or a frog.

I have a mane,
But not a very good brain,
I am the king of the jungle
And when you hear my belly rumble,
You know it's time to run,
I'll eat you and your mum.

A lion.

Fars Saleh & Zoe Alexandra Irving (11)
Heavers Farm Primary School, South Norwood

Animals

I love animals
They are ever so sweet
Some prance, some jump
Some creep, some run.

Some look hideous
While some look cute
Some look red and hot all over
And some look pale white, like paper
While some look pink, like candyfloss.

They come in all different colours, shapes and sizes
Every single plant and animal
Come in all different varieties.

If you go into a jungle
And you see a creature, plant or animal . . .

Don't scream or shout.
Just hold your breath
And that will help you out.

If you decide to take the wrong turn
Let me give you a piece of advice
Do not get carried away
And throw your hand upon them
Because if you bark up the wrong tree
They just bark right back down!

Monique Vanessa Bailey-McKenzie (11)
Heavers Farm Primary School, South Norwood

My Favourite Animals

As blind as a bat,
As fun as a cat,
As dumb as a starfish,
As soft as a sponge.

I'm fond of fast animals,
Peregrine falcons, cheetahs too,
I like meat-eaters, they're very fierce,
Most of them are big, you'd better fear.

Animals, animals, they are so fun,
Animals, animals, they're so big,
Animals, some smaller than your thumb,
Animals, the smallest even hum.

As slimy as a slug,
As sneaky as a snake,
As slow as a snail,
As thick as a worm.

I'm also fond of furry animals,
Guinea pigs, hamsters, gnus,
I also like monkeys, they're furry too.

A world without animals,
Wouldn't be as much fun,
Animals, animals!
Don't shoot them with a gun!

Joshua Brown (11)
Heavers Farm Primary School, South Norwood

My Animal Poem

Silky cat padding softly on the floor,
Quietly creeping past the door,
Where I was stood before,
Furry and big, standing tall,
Then later laying lazily with a ball.

Slippery dolphins diving through the air,
Where they go they don't care,
Suddenly splashing water everywhere,
Later they lay softly there.

Dogs are cute and kind,
With a lovely, lovely caring mind,
Cuddly and sweet, they sit tall and stand high
Walking in a straight line.

Soft rabbit warm and small,
It runs round the garden like a bull,
Then later it feels silky and like some wool,
Later it is curled up so small.

Rebecca Donnelly (10)
Heavers Farm Primary School, South Norwood

The Hunter

Blasting through the grass like a rocket,
Fierce but soft as a pocket,
His prey is antelope,
How can he cope
With an antelope down his throat?

He's got it, he won't let go
His cubs come out slow,
The antelope's struggling,
The cubs are arguing,
At the meat they are tugging.

David Layne (11)
Heavers Farm Primary School, South Norwood

Animals, Animals

Leopard
Leopard, leopard runs so fast,
Leopard, leopard you can't get past,
Leopard, leopard don't try to mess,
Leopard, leopard they are the best.

Frog
My frog is like a bouncy castle,
It jumps, it hops, it sleeps, it leaps,
Now it looks like it could do with something to eat!

Bear
The bear is big,
The bear is fat,
The bear looks like an angry cat,
He brushes his teeth with a bristly twig.

Elephant
Elephant, elephant scared of a mouse,
Elephant, elephant as big as a house,
Elephant, elephant as strong as tornado,
Elephant, elephant just watch the way it flows.

Charnae Thompson-Grey (11)
Heavers Farm Primary School, South Norwood

Sad Snake

The sad snake sat, smoothly singing sadly,
Then the stupid, silly scorpion sank softly in the sea.
Along came the sleepy spider who sailed the ship
All of a sudden, the slimy slug and snail came slowly by
They all go by as the sad snake is sitting smoothly singing sadly.

Kemi Oyekan
Heavers Farm Primary School, South Norwood

My Animals

My leopard
My leopard is like a furry dotted rug
All it does is swallow bugs
It sleeps and snores
It shakes the floors
I love to cuddle my leopard.

My Frog
My frog is like a bouncing ball
It jumps, it leaps
What did I give it to eat?

My Bear
My bear is like a fat cushion
It roars
It's a bother
Oh no, I think he's about to eat my mother!

Tanika Silbourne-Martin (10)
Heavers Farm Primary School, South Norwood

Guess Who?

Big pointy nose
Skinny and wears black
Big hooked nose
Rides on a broom
Bad and magical
Small creaky voice
Stinky and smelly
Who is it?

Answer: a witch.

Gabriel Bakare (8)
Heavers Farm Primary School, South Norwood

Animals

Cheetah
Cheetah, cheetah, near or far,
I can see you wherever you are.
If there's one thing I know,
You're the best cheetah I've ever known.

Cuddly bear
Cuddly bear sitting there,
Thank you for stopping all my fear.
When I'm asleep I think of you,
So never go away, whatever you do.

Dolphin
Dolphin, dolphin, swimming bright,
Why can't you be with me all night?
When I watch you it calms me down,
So whatever you do, don't let me down!

Little rabbit
Little rabbit, in its burrow,
Sleeping quietly, on a pillow.
Don't wake it up or it'll have a fright
And run away out of sight.

Kymara Jackson & Bansri Shah (10)
Heavers Farm Primary School, South Norwood

Dog

Cat catcher
Glass smasher
Water drinker
Fast runner
Great swimmer
Hard biter
Far jumper
Bone cruncher.

Markus Barrow (9)
Heavers Farm Primary School, South Norwood

Animals

Big cows moo loudly
Little cows moo softly
Like a song in the sky
Eating juicy green grass down below.

Hunting fox hops slowly in our garden
While we sleep at night-time
Killing rats and cats,
Rabbits are down in the dark ground.

Sleeping cat purrs loudly
In my bedroom
Crawls to his food
Down in the kitchen.

Two swans a-swimming
In the warm summer air
Up the river, down the river
Two is company
Two is a pair.

Amy Dean (10)
Heavers Farm Primary School, South Norwood

Guess Who?

Cat hater
Loud barker
Toy chewer
Biscuit biter
Water drinker
Carpet roller
Tail chaser
Tongue roller.

Answer: dog.

Melissa Zulu (8)
Heavers Farm Primary School, South Norwood

Animal Poem

Easter bunny
Easter bunny in the fresh green spring,
Watching the farmer grow his vegetables,
Steals a carrot and to him that's what spring brings.

Dolphin
As the dolphin sinks down into deep waters,
Watch the glistening water on its back,
It has approached the water in the dim dark black.

Four-minute-old kitten
A new kitten is born into the world
And his first sound is *miaow*
He is wrapped in a towel
Four-minute-old kittens are amazing.

Jellyfish
Dynamic jellyfish crazy tentacles
Don't agitate it or you will be stung
Would you go back?
I wouldn't, not me!

Rena Gwasaze (11)
Heavers Farm Primary School, South Norwood

Animals

Five little squirrels sat up in a tree
The first one said, 'What can I see?'
The first said again, 'A man with a gun.'
The second one said, 'Then we'd better run!'
The third one said, 'Let's hide in the shade.'
The fourth one said, 'I'm not afraid!'
The fifth one saw the man with the gun,
Then *bang* went the gun and how they did run!

Kayley Bennett (10)
Heavers Farm Primary School, South Norwood

Animals

Flying birds hovering in the sky
Looking for wriggly worms
As they're passing by.

Sleepy leopard sleeping heavily
However, he is poorly
And his name is Rory.

Blue dolphin jumping up and down
As he splashes and splashes
Leaving trails of water around.

Smooth furry cat
Licks the bowl of milk
And creeps to her favourite mat.

Afiya Shameela Muir (11)
Heavers Farm Primary School, South Norwood

Animals

Horses
Look at the horses
Eating the hay greedily
Mother horse is coming
Let's run away speedily.

Goldfish
I have two goldfish
They swim very proudly
And their fins go swish
But ever so loudly!

Kitten
Look at that kitten
It's ever so cute
It's a shame they don't wear mittens
It would make a suit.

Louise Marquis (10)
Heavers Farm Primary School, South Norwood

The Colours Of The World

Blue for the sky,
Blue for the sea,
Blue for the butterfly looking at me.

Orange for the sun,
Orange for fire,
Orange for the topaz that men desire.

Brown for earth beneath our feet,
Brown for the wheat, I do eat.

White for the clouds up in the sky,
White for the snowy peaks that stretch so high.

But the most important to me,
Are the colours of land and sea,
In the colours of the rainbow,
Staring at me!

Charlie Antony Spittle (9)
Heavers Farm Primary School, South Norwood

Animals

A fast jaguar
I have the name of a car
I'm as fast as a car
I am a bolt of lightning
So fast, you can't name your sighting
I'm someone you can't record
I'm faster than a Honda Accord
I'm a really . . . flash cat!

Sarmad Suhail (10)
Heavers Farm Primary School, South Norwood

Dogs

Barking dog
Howling loudly
Chasing cats
Frightening people
Causing trouble
All the time
My dog sleeps
Like a big fat cat
All the time
That's why I
Like my dog so much
The dog next door
Jumps up at the fence
And then my dog
Starts barking
In defence.

Dermorneay Pinnock (10)
Heavers Farm Primary School, South Norwood

My Little Black Dog

Fast as a cheetah he runs up the hill
Never once has he kept still,
Fluffy as a cat
Obediently he sat.

Dark as midnight
Never once has he lost sight
Of bones and biscuits
That he likes.

Then he starts to chase
Barking and catching the cat
Frightening people and the bat.

Robert Eccleston (10)
Heavers Farm Primary School, South Norwood

Party In The Club

Here we go,
Come on, yo'
Move your body up
Move it down
Keep doing that till you get down town
You leave your kids at home
And call the babysitter on the phone.
Then yo' enter the club
By turning on the knob
And put your junk in the bin
'What you going to do with all that junk
All that junk inside your trunk?'
Then move your body up, move it down
Shake your body and turn around
And then you just drop to the ground
Party all night and evening
Get that pulse rate beating
Nobody takes a sea and no one's eating
Then go home to the kids and say, 'Babysitter leave,
Or your pay you don't receive.'
And that's what you done
From zero to hero
Oh my days, you're Heaven's son.

Ayomide Lawal (9)
Heavers Farm Primary School, South Norwood

Anti-Bullying

A bully is a guy
Who likes throwing pie,
He walks with a gang,
Hits with a *bang!*
To stop this bully
Just say *no!*
Tell an adult
What you know!

Arslaan Ahmed (10)
Heavers Farm Primary School, South Norwood

Crazy Ape

Crazy ape trying to escape from the steel cage
By bashing, punching, biting, kicking,
Smashing, crashing, scrunching,
Pulverising, crushing, battering,
The steel bars trying to open them
To return to his home jungle and friends
Which are a bird and a cat.

Fat cat who sleeps on a mat
Getting a snack in his dream
Thinking of some cream.

Quick bird flying in a bright flight
Trying to seek scraps for its children
So they sleep tight at night.

Asad Mahmood (10)
Heavers Farm Primary School, South Norwood

Anti-Bullying

When somebody is getting bullied
I'm not very pleased,
Because they're getting teased.
They all are mad
And the other people get sad
I want to stop this
So help me do it!

Ryan Bio-Genfi (9)
Heavers Farm Primary School, South Norwood

Haiku

Dogs dashing so fast
Dogs dashing through the park fast
Sprinting fast for food.

Stuart Adams (10)
Heavers Farm Primary School, South Norwood

Bat, Cat

Terrified bat
Scared of the bright light
Flying cave to cave
Until it is night

Flying birds in bright flight
Seeking snacks for its rumbling belly
So it can sleep tight all night

Fat cat sleeps on a mat
Ready to get a snack after his nap
In his dream, thinking of cream.

Aaron Kirson (11)
Heavers Farm Primary School, South Norwood

Just Like . . .

A winding rope just like a snake,
Slithers slowly just like a snail,
Don't touch, maybe you'll be its next prey.

A jumping Jack just like a frog,
Bouncy just like a ball,
Don't bring one in your home, it might leave a trail.

Shavaneese Grant (10)
Heavers Farm Primary School, South Norwood

Say No!

Say no to anybody who tries to bully you,
If they do, you know who to go to,
Stand up to them and get this stopped,
Instead of getting into a fight and getting dropped,
Now you know what to do,
If someone tries to bully you.

Muka Zimba (9)
Heavers Farm Primary School, South Norwood

I Would Like To Be . . .

Shapes and patterns on the wing,
Flying gracefully over everything,
Sunshine buttery yellow and bright,
Everyone wants to have a sight,
Delicate and small,
Gliding swiftly, away from a rolling ball
A butterfly, not right at all.

Tail like a spinning fan,
Jumping wildly at the sausages in the pan,
Mischievous and fun,
Laying down in the sun,
Rubbing your soggy nose on my face,
Beating me in a race,
A dog, not right at all.

Digging a burrow, long and muddy,
Humungous ears and very cuddly,
Hopping around the flowers in the field,
You are very strong-willed,
Soft and smooth,
Always on the move,
A rabbit, not right at all.

Soft and furry, is you, the cat,
Curled up on the mat,
Claws as sharp as a razorblade,
Lying down in the shade,
Muddy paw prints on the floor,
Hole in the carpet, you've had a gnaw,
Trying to catch a bird's wing,
I wish I were you, because you can get away with anything.

Catherine Prescott (11)
Heavers Farm Primary School, South Norwood

Bullying

Make the right choice,
Listen to the right voice,
Don't let the bullies run the show,
I know when to say yes and no.
I've got the willpower to try and say no,
Everyone will support me wherever I go,
Here is a message just for you,
Follow the advice to help you through.
I want the bullying to stop,
So then we can all be at the top.
If I've got the willpower,
So have you!
The bullies are gone
Because I've proved them wrong!

Jasmine Jutlay (9)
Heavers Farm Primary School, South Norwood

Say No!

Don't listen to bullies in the street,
Say no! Look away from them.
Don't listen to what they say,
'Cause you're better anyway.

You can tell a little joke to your friend,
Be careful of what you say,
You don't want your friendship to end.

Don't listen to bullies in the street,
Say no! Look away from them.

Sian Brizelden (9)
Heavers Farm Primary School, South Norwood

Stop!

Leave me alone!
I'm proud of myself,
I will learn to fight battles,
But not on my own.
Tell a teacher
She'll come and meet ya
Perhaps you have a problem
That's troubling you;
We'll try and help you
And show you what to do.

Imani Awodipe (9)
Heavers Farm Primary School, South Norwood

What Is . . . Water?

Water is a flying saucepan travelling through silky oil
Water is a shining silk floating down the drain
Water is a shining, glittery mirror on a hot day
Water is a Ripple chocolate bar on top of a Dairy Milk.
Water is floating jelly bouncing up and down a trillion times.

Jack George West (9)
Kingswood Primary School, Lower Kingswood

What Is . . . Water?

Water is melted chocolate in a giant's bowl
The water is a wave growing over the rocks
Water is a giant volcano bubbling like a hot bath
Water is rotten cabbage on bright blue tarpaulin
Water is a swirling, whirling, whirlpool going down the plughole.

James Fitzwalter (9)
Kingswood Primary School, Lower Kingswood

A Rhyming Poem

Monday's child likes to stay
Tuesday's child likes to play
Wednesday's child likes to watch telly
Thursday's child likes to eat jelly
Friday's child likes to eat chips
Saturday's child likes to lick their lips
But the child that is born on the Sabbath Day
Likes to play a different way.

Sophie Thomas (6)
Kingswood Primary School, Lower Kingswood

What Is . . . Water?

It is an unleashed power, roaming around in the sky
Water is magic in the air, flying about
It is a candle that shines so brightly at night, in the sky
It is blue waves made by flying horses in the sky
It is hot lava spouting out of an exploding volcano.

Ella Smeddles (9)
Kingswood Primary School, Lower Kingswood

What Is . . . Water?

Water is money dropped on a hard table, rolling around
Water is babies' fingers gently tapping me
Water is a leaf falling down on an autumn afternoon
Water is children shouting in the playground, smiling
Water is a parachute drifting gently out of a trickling tap.

Holly Wayman (9)
Kingswood Primary School, Lower Kingswood

A Rhyming Poem

Monday's child likes to play
Tuesday's child likes to stay
Wednesday's child likes to leap
Thursday's child likes to sleep
Friday's child likes to peep
Saturday's child likes to creep
But the child who was born on the Sabbath day
Likes to play in a different way.

Libby Moy (7)
Kingswood Primary School, Lower Kingswood

What Is . . . Water

Water is a mirror reflecting day or night
Water is a clear window on a misty day
Water is an erupting volcano bursting hot lava
Water is dark shadows moving across silver skies
Water is glass but cracks to make ripples that reflect in the sky.

Hannah Rhian Milbourn (9)
Kingswood Primary School, Lower Kingswood

What Is . . . Water?

Water is stones dropped from the sky into some hot trousers, boiled
Water is a wavy hair shone on a playground
Water is a foot stumped on an open space, with a wallop
Water is a foot grumbling on the path, a shaking earthquake
Water is a raindrop falling from a child's eye onto the ground.

Melissa Cooper (9)
Kingswood Primary School, Lower Kingswood

Monday's Child

Monday's child likes to be a pain
Tuesday's child likes to play in the rain
Wednesday's child likes to play
Thursday's child likes to go on holiday
Friday's child is a guy
Saturday's child likes pie
But the child that's born on the Sabbath day
Likes to lay.

James Cox (6)
Kingswood Primary School, Lower Kingswood

What Is . . . Water?

The pond is a big dark shadow moulded like a giant's head
The pond is a Mars bar with ripples on the top
It is a rumble of volcanoes erupting
It is a melting ice cream that's dripping from the cone
The water is a plate of blackcurrant jelly that hasn't set.

Hayley Sandalls (9)
Kingswood Primary School, Lower Kingswood

What Is . . . Water?

Water is green cabbage on top of murky cold beef soup
It is some chewing gum on the wheel of your bicycle
The water is brown ripples on a melted, delicious Mars bar
Water is blackcurrants squashed in a juicer machine
Water looks like silk ribbons twirling like a shiny whirlpool.

Carmen Cheung (9)
Kingswood Primary School, Lower Kingswood

What Is . . . Water?

The pond is a great big shadow from a giant in Heaven
Water dripping is chewing gum on a bike wheel
The fountain is a snake, of course in a lot of grass
The water maker is a volcano erupting
The pond is a revolting, gigantic, repugnant blackcurrant jelly.

Amy Elise Parfitt (9)
Kingswood Primary School, Lower Kingswood

What Is . . . Water?

Water is a rippling waterfall of stars
Water is tapping fingers
The pond is a blackcurrant jelly with cream on top
Water is a rumbling dinosaur
Water is a black margherita pizza.

Peter Culff (9)
Kingswood Primary School, Lower Kingswood

Seals Can . . .

Seals can . . .
S-l-i-d-e
Eat fish
Swim
Wave
Slap
Play ball
Talk
B-a-l-a-n-c-e balls
Seals!

Charlotte Godwin (7)
Kingswood Primary School, Lower Kingswood

What Is . . . Water?

Water is a massive wave falling from a gigantic cloud
It is melted chocolate with ripples on top
It is a colossal, hot, rumbling volcano erupting
It is a fifty metre slithering, scaly snake
It is thousands of horses sailing across the big, blue, wide sky.

Jessie Catherine Juliana Scott (9)
Kingswood Primary School, Lower Kingswood

What Is . . . Water?

Water is a spider falling out of a drain
Water is a floating cage of mystical things
Water is a piece of DNA on fire
Water is a boom of grey spirits falling from the sky
Water is an explosion of blue
Water is a slide of liquid.

James Leach (9)
Kingswood Primary School, Lower Kingswood

What Is . . . Water?

The fountain is a gushing mini waterfall which you drink
The water fountain is smoke coming from a bomb
The boiler is a colossal, bubbling hot pool of lava
The boiler is a massive red erupting volcano
Water is a transparent mirror travelling every second.

Matthew Gray (9)
Kingswood Primary School, Lower Kingswood

What Is . . . Water?

Water is a boiling tap and a rumbling, smashing earthquake
Water is a large swimming pool of blackcurrants
Water is shiny, glittery mirrors on a hot evening
Water is ripples on top of Mars bars that are brown
The water is a calm, relaxing, midsummer morning at noon.

Neeve Marnie Pearce (9)
Kingswood Primary School, Lower Kingswood

What Is . . . Water?

Water is a shiny mirror in the sun with gorgeous gold
It is a glorious hint of rainbow colours
It is a magnificent crystal clear picture of glimmer
It is a ballet shoe with ribbon trickling slowly
It is a sparkling glittering ripple with chocolate coming.

Olivia Mae Gleaves (9)
Kingswood Primary School, Lower Kingswood

What Is . . . Water?

It is a big, fat, green, yummy jelly on a shiny plate
It is an erupting volcano of lava
Water is a bluish pool of smelly toxic waste
Water is a giant mirror on a big round frame
Water is a blasting machine gun of destruction and terror.

Samuel Cowlam (9)
Kingswood Primary School, Lower Kingswood

What Is . . . Water?

The water is my sister's dirty hair on a Sunday night
The reeds are cabbage floating in a hot saucepan
Water is blue, rumbling and erupting volcano lava
The hot water is hissing like a snake's hiss
The water is the calm ripples of the chocolate on a Mars bar.

Daniel Gillbanks (9)
Kingswood Primary School, Lower Kingswood

What Is . . . Water?

It is a giant mirror reflecting the shady grey sky
It is a giant lump of wobbling plain jelly
It is an enormous, dark, sinister, grey, scary shadow
It is a giant's sweat gland on a day that is hot
It is a pizza with black dough, disgusting French snails
And green herbs.

James Evans (9)
Kingswood Primary School, Lower Kingswood

What Is . . . Water?

A pond is a cheese and garlic pizza about to be eaten
A pond is a cool shadow on a hard brick wall
A pond is a steaming hot big bath in a bubbly bathroom
A pond is a rough big bed cover in a bedroom
A pond is a giant ugly pool
With soft blackcurrant jelly in it.

Leah Pearson (9)
Kingswood Primary School, Lower Kingswood

An Acrostic Poem

B irds fly round in circles
I n a cage they are playful
R acing together
D angling their wings
S wooping everywhere.

Sophie Goodenough (6)
Kingswood Primary School, Lower Kingswood

An Acrostic Poem

W olves can climb up willow trees
O ooowww is the sound they make
L ick litter
V ery vicious
E at rabbits
S ometimes scare human beings.

James Cowlam (7)
Kingswood Primary School, Lower Kingswood

An Acrostic Poem

W hales swim at the bottom
H ate sharks
A lways dive
L ike fish
E at meat
S wim very fast.

Kasharna Williams (6)
Kingswood Primary School, Lower Kingswood

What Is . . . Water?

Water is a wiggling, whirling whirlpool that ripples up and down
Water is the stars at night bursting rapidly
Water is a place in Heaven, splishing and splashing madly
Water is explosions bursting all over the wild
Water is a volcanic eruption
Is that alright with you?

Sam Paul Dobell (9)
Kingswood Primary School, Lower Kingswood

An Acrostic Poem

T igers tickle their toes
I n a cage they are afraid
G rrrrrr is the noise they make
E ating animals
R ushing tigers
S noozy tigers.

Carys Milbourn (7)
Kingswood Primary School, Lower Kingswood

Acrostic Poem

P igs love mud
I n a sty they live
G et happy in the mud
S nout for their noses.

Naomi Crane (6)
Kingswood Primary School, Lower Kingswood

Gymnastics

Here we go it's warm-up, time to loosen up my joints
I've got to do my somersaults so that I can score some points.
Up I get, off I step and to the mat I go
I've got to jump and twist about and put on a super show.
The track rumbles as I hurtle into a tumble
You gets lots of ticks as you round off flicks.
I balance on blocks and my legs tightly lock
So I look at the clock as it goes tick-tock.
I hope you enjoyed it, I did my best, I hope I did it well
If I end up on the podium it will make me feel so swell.

Paris Scott-Waller (10)
Newington CE Primary School, Sittingbourne

I'd Rather Be . . .

I'd rather be in Spain than here,
I'd rather be a tiger than a deer,
I'd rather say yes than maybe,
I'd rather be a child than a baby,
I'd rather eat pizza than pork,
I'd rather be an eagle than a hawk,
I'd rather be happy than sad,
I'd rather be me than my dad,
I'd rather be a dog than a rat,
I'd rather wear a coat than a hat,
I'd rather be clever than barmy,
I'd rather drink beer than barley,
I've now come to the end of my poem,
Because I have got to do the mowing.

Richard Jeffrey (9)
Newington CE Primary School, Sittingbourne

My Wicked Rap

My name is Lewis Howes
And I have loads of pals
I come from the west
And I love a rest
I always stay awake
When I eat cake
Whenever I drink wine
I stay up till nine
I like Bart
Because he is smart
Whenever I cry
I look at the sky
I'm not very tall
And I hate shopping malls.

Lewis Howes (10)
Newington CE Primary School, Sittingbourne

My Cats

Sharp teeth, like razors
Long claws, ready to attack
Smirky face, up to something
Prowling, creeping towards me.

Eyes so bright, like the moonlight
Stripy coat, like a tiger
Slowly walking, like a tortoise
And then out of nowhere
Ready, ready, *pounce!*

Natasha Elliott (9)
Newington CE Primary School, Sittingbourne

A Recipe For Trouble
Getting Sent To The Head Teacher

You will need nothing, except a head teacher,
Yourself, a few random objects from the classroom
And a few friends (or an audience).

Start by cracking some jokes and afterwards
Mix them with some melted laughter;

Put them aside for a while
And start flicking some pens and pencils,
She'll be in denial;

Stage three would be to . . .
Make it obvious you're pretending you've got the flu;

For the finishing touches,
Try tripping a few people up,
One of them might end up on crutches;

Walk out of the room to go to the head,
With a bit of disappointment,
Or try laughing instead.

Carrie-Ann Bevan
Newington CE Primary School, Sittingbourne

Love

L ighting up people's hearts
O verwhelming desire
V ery happy times
E motions glistening in the moonlight!

Shauna Westlake (10)
Newington CE Primary School, Sittingbourne

Hallowe'en

The moon is out,
The sky is black.
You can see a silhouette
Of a witch's cat.

On Hallowe'en you can hear screaming
And footsteps running about.
In the graveyard, zombies arise,
To scare the children and give them a surprise.

You can hear werewolves howling
In the dark misty night.
Dogs are growling,
When the children go by.

Mummies arise from their tombs,
With insects and bandages hanging from their necks.
Skeletons pop out of nowhere,
Frightening people to death!

Liam Ingram
Newington CE Primary School, Sittingbourne

A Dark Night

The stars are out
And the sound of screaming
Runs through my ears

I can see flowing orbs
I can hear a wolf howling

Zombies rising, eating people alive
Frankenstein hypnotises the old nannies
Ghosts take over their bodies.

Reece Ingram
Newington CE Primary School, Sittingbourne

Sharnie

S harnie is what this poem is about
H annah is my best friend
A nyone who knows me is my friend
R abbits are my favourite animal
N ever think for myself
I s always on the run
E ight is my lucky number!

Sharnie Yiannari
Newington CE Primary School, Sittingbourne

Sea Poem

Look at the glistening sea,
With the wind sweeping away your fears,
The calming current to relax your body,
Reminding you of the life you have.
The waves bringing happiness,
The smell of the sea salt taking away your anger,
That's my idea of the sea.

Zoe-Jayne Barber (10)
Newington CE Primary School, Sittingbourne

Alliteration

Terrible tortoise tearing teabags
Troubled tigers trying to trip
Thrushes throwing things
Fish fighting for food
Flying fortresses firing fire
Six slimy snakes squirming
Seven slippy slugs sliding
Eight elephants excavating
Nine naughty nails nicking newts
Terrible tarantulas tearing towns down.

James Wood (10)
Newington CE Primary School, Sittingbourne

What Sport?

Twenty-two players explore the pitch as they play this sport,
The ball gets passed up and down the colossal green floor,
Until the ball rolls into the vast mouth,
The crowd all cheer, Arsenal win the game again,
The game is over,
Yeah, yeah, yeah,
My team has won,
Go, go Arsenal!

Samantha Crook (10)
Newington CE Primary School, Sittingbourne

Sadness

I look down the river
Only see black and white
Then grey emerges
It has no right.

The water is murky
Like my feelings inside
I am sad
But no one cares.

Ellen Pinnock (10)
Newington CE Primary School, Sittingbourne

A Gorilla

G orillas are so hairy
O r sometimes they're quite scary
R unning about at night
I n the darkness they're so small
L ike a big fat chimpanzee
L ike a great big fat spot
A nd it might even eat me.

Spencer Wanstall (10)
Newington CE Primary School, Sittingbourne

Shape Poem

S and is yellow like the sun
H airs are thin or thick, or a *hare* is fast
A lligators have sharp pointy teeth like knives
P ears are nice to eat
E lephants are big and heavy

P eople are nice to be around
O ctopus is nice and slimy
E mus are big birds with long legs
M onkeys are naughty and funny.

Sarah Baker (10)
Newington CE Primary School, Sittingbourne

The Sea

The sea
Peaceful and quiet
Making you fall asleep
A blue blanket moving slowly
So slow

The sea
A peaceful place
So lovely
Just watching it is wonderful
The sea.

Bronwen Barton (10)
Newington CE Primary School, Sittingbourne

Love

Love is a pale pink
Love is a feeling from deep inside
Love is a passion you cannot hide
Love is like chocolate melting in your mouth.

Kayleigh Mersh (10)
Newington CE Primary School, Sittingbourne

Hunger

Hunger kills, hunger hurts,
Hunger strikes the hearts of countries,
It takes the lives of others,
Taking lives means taking hearts,
Hunger kills the Earth, bit by bit.

It is a black hole, taking all that lives on Earth,
The whole world is gradually dying,
The whole world is dying of . . .
Hunger!

Luke Hipkiss
Newington CE Primary School, Sittingbourne

Something Is Under My Bed

Something is crawling under my bed,
I feel it creeping beneath me.

I can smell its odour, clear and strong,
Something is under my bed.

I can hear its whistles, right in my ear,
Something is under my bed.

I feel the bumps and scales on its skin,
Something is under my bed!

Emma Jennings (11)
Newington CE Primary School, Sittingbourne

I'd Like To Be . . .

If I were a vegetable, I'd like to be a carrot
But if I were an animal, I'd like to be a lizard
If I were a movie star, I'd like to be Johnny Depp
If I had the chance, I'd like to be Tony Hawk
But still, I just like being me!

Charlie Chalmers
Newington CE Primary School, Sittingbourne

Seasons

Springtime
New life appears
Blossom falls from the trees
Everyone admires flowers
Springtime.

Summer
Lovely hot sun
People head to the beach
Everyone eats melting ice creams
Summer.

Autumn
Leaves are falling
Conkers fall to the ground
Red, gold and brown leaves fall from trees
Autumn.

Winter
Snow starts to fall
Build snowmen with the snow
Stick your tongue out and feel the snow
Winter.

Daisy-Mae Cole (10)
Newington CE Primary School, Sittingbourne

The Willow Tree

The leaves flutter in the wind,
It's like hair waving in the wind,
It's like ribbons falling down to the ground,
The willow tree.

Shooting up like fireworks,
Brushes like falling hair,
The singing out loud now,
It's time to whisper like a mouse,
The willow tree, the willow tree,
There's nothing like the willow tree.

Natasha Roome
Newington CE Primary School, Sittingbourne

Playtime

The bell has gone,
We're out to play,
Come on everyone,
It's hot today!

Let's play football,
Let's play catch,
Come on, don't dawdle,
Come on, don't scratch!

They decide on catch,
They run around,
They think about a match,
As the ball twirls on the ground.

The end of play,
The whistle's blown,
They stand and say,
'I've got a brand new ringtone!'

Annabel West
Newington CE Primary School, Sittingbourne

Hallowe'en

Hallowe'en is time for witches,
Flying in the sky on their broomsticks,
Ghosts and ghouls covered with stitches,
Nasty children play their tricks,

Devils dressed all red and scary,
Darkness covered with red splattered blood,
Children's masks made all hairy,
Witches landing with a thud.

Children running in the streets,
Dressed to scare, but also have fun,
Happy and excited with all their treats,
Creeping home when the night is done.

Michaela Hearnden (10)
Newington CE Primary School, Sittingbourne

Black Night Horse

Black night horse sniffs the air
Kick in the side
He's gone.
Black night horse leaves marks in the mud
Sounds of the whip
He's gone.
Black night horse twitches, flicks
Smell of people
He's gone.
Black night horse has a rider
They have dark brown eyes and hair
That rider is me.
Black night horse canters down the lane
Slap of the reins
He's gone.

Eleanor Skelton (9)
Newington CE Primary School, Sittingbourne

Sirens

On the beach you see him blowing,
See him going and flowing,
To the pebbles he goes,
You can see him gallop across the sand,
Watch him take a bath in the sea.
Sirens.

In his stable, the moon shines on him so plain,
His hay is crispy, like sweet grain,
For in the meadow, the grass is damp from all the rain.
In the schooling ring, there is no grass at all,
Look into the jumping arena, it is all the grass you will ever need.
Sirens.

Matilda Butler (10)
Newington CE Primary School, Sittingbourne

Bonfire Night

Bonfire Night,
Bonfire Night,
When the sky has a sight
And I have a fright
On that night.

When I go to the bonfire
To see it burn
And I burnt
My mum's fern.

Bonfire Night,
Bonfire Night,
When the sky has a sight
And I have a fright
On that night.

Guy Fawkes goes up in flames
As I chucked on some games
And my little trains.

Jack Dennison (10)
Newington CE Primary School, Sittingbourne

Dolphins

D olphins play happily
O ctopus floating in the sea
L azy fish too
P acific Ocean flows beautifully
H igh above there are seagulls
I n the sea, stingrays on the bottom
N aughty sharks play angry games
S tingrays look for some nice food.

Reece Garrett (10)
Newington CE Primary School, Sittingbourne

My Dad

My dad, with his bulging belly,
He eats all the jelly,
How loud are his snores?
He only hears what he wants,
The rest, he ignores!
When he drinks in the pub,
It sounds like *glub, glub, glub!*
He's my dad and I'm glad!

Sophie Barton (9)
Newington CE Primary School, Sittingbourne

The Willow Tree

Swaying in the wind,
You can swing on it, like Tarzan,
A good place to hide in,
The willow tree.

Green leaves swing around,
Like a girl's bad hair day,
Singing with the wind,
The willow tree.

Grant Rawlinson
Newington CE Primary School, Sittingbourne

Chas

C has is not a chav
H e is a great skater
A lways raring to go
S kating is his life.

Chas Beacock (11)
Newington CE Primary School, Sittingbourne

Leprechaun

L ittle green men with pots of gold
E ars sticking up, looking bold
P eople cannot get his shillings
R un away, there might be killings
E vil tricks to be used
C ome away, you might get bruised
H ere he comes, with his bride
A nd she can run, but she can't hide
U nder the stairs, under the bed
N obody knows if he's in your head!

Toby North (11)
Newington CE Primary School, Sittingbourne

Winter Tree

My twisted branches all battered and old
The blizzard-like wind stripped away the leaves I once had
I look back at when I was once strong
As my life comes to an end
I let the snow cover me like a shroud
I hope my children grow to see as many glorious moments as I did
I shut my eyes and go to sleep.

Ryan Underwood (9)
Penns Primary School, Sutton Coldfield

A Tree In Winter

I am an old tree now
My roots are like twisted, crumpled paper
I am no longer beautiful
My leaves are crushed like shattered glass
I feel the soft snow cover me
Now I will pass peacefully away.

Reah Ashmore-Brown (9)
Penns Primary School, Sutton Coldfield

A Tree In Winter

Old wrinkly bark
Where, once before, soft, smooth skin
Oh, how I wish, how much I wish
It was spring again.

In the spring my seeds fell to the ground
The seeds are my children
The first to shoot up, my boys
The last, my girls.

In the summer I looked my best
Young, strong and healthy
I danced in the wind's gentle breeze
But now I am old.

In the autumn I was middle-aged
Branches starting to creak
Leaves turning brown and tumbling to the ground
How I wish I was young again.

But now winter has come
I want to sleep, sleep and never wake
I hope my children are proud of me
The wise old tree with the snow as my shroud.

Katie Edwards (9)
Penns Primary School, Sutton Coldfield

A Tree In Winter

My twisted branches are as old as the very first tree
My bark is no use now
My leaves have been blown away by the autumn wind.
I remember when children used to swing on my branches
Those were the good days
Now the snow covers me like a shroud
But ahead, there is the life of my seeds
They will grow strong and beautiful, like I used to be.
Winter has come
It is the end of my life.

Ethan Cunniffe (9)
Penns Primary School, Sutton Coldfield

A Tree In Winter

The world no longer needs me
My branches droop to the ground
My gnarled bark is delicate and crumbles
As I whisper my secrets to the saplings.

The world no longer needs me
The wind to me is no longer a sugary-sweet solo
That I can dance to in the bitter breeze
It's now sour salt.

The world no longer needs me
I'll wait until I freeze in my icy coffin
The winter will pass
And I will be gone.

The world no longer needs me.

Elizabeth Barrett (9)
Penns Primary School, Sutton Coldfield

A Tree In Winter

In spring I blossom and children climb me
In autumn my leaves go brown and crunchy
In winter my bark crumbles and falls
The snow rests on my branches
All I have done, is all I want to do
So I'll close my eyes with many memories
And never open them again
Smaller trees will grow from my seeds
It will be the same for them
Now the winter has ended
No more will I see the world change
My time has come to sleep.

Imogen Withers (9)
Penns Primary School, Sutton Coldfield

A Tree In Winter

I know my youth is fading away
Oh how I wish I could sway and dance to the wind's song again.
All knobbly and stiff, my wrinkled bark is crumbling
Oh how children used to climb and swing about upon my branches.
In the summer, people gathered in my shade for picnics
They admired my colourful blossoms
How beautiful I was then!
I could stand up straight and proud!
How weak and ugly I am now
I feel so very useless.
I am at the end of my life
All my memories are passing by as the snow softly falls.

Tilly Christie-Thompson (9)
Penns Primary School, Sutton Coldfield

A Tree In Winter

I once was a young noble tree
But my smooth roots
Are now gnarled
My bark, all wrinkled and old.
When I was young
People would stop and look up at my magnificent leaves
But now there are none left to see
They have all slowly drifted away in the autumn breeze.
Children would hang on my branches
But now I am too fragile
I am looking forward to calmly going to sleep
Never again to wake.

Celine Dowd (9)
Penns Primary School, Sutton Coldfield

Little Old Lady

Little old lady sitting there,
Staring out to the world
From her dilapidated window
As white as a ghost
Waiting for someone to come to her
To look after her.

Never will we see her lights go off or her curtains close
As still as the squirrel perching in her garden
She hardly moves
Eventually she will rot like a discarded apple.

She watches the day pass her by
Waiting for someone
Just anyone
To notice her.

Clara Matty (10)
Penns Primary School, Sutton Coldfield

My Grandpa

Grandpa's hands were as rough as coal
His hands were as warm as a fire
Wrapping my hands and squeezing like a snake.

Grandpa's hair was as grey as the moon
He had beady eyes that sparkled like a sapphire
I love my grandpa
I miss him every moment.

Timothy Ind (9)
Penns Primary School, Sutton Coldfield

A Tree In Winter

I have watched things change
Over the years of my age,
My leaves disappear into thin air
And my branches are broken, till there is nothing left.

I feel so useless,
For I used to shelter squirrels and birds
And children in summer storms,
But now my colourful leaves are gone
And I can't do anything at all.

In my youth,
Children climbed on my strong branches
And I held them safely,
But my branches are too weak for that,
I fall at the slightest touch.

The winter snow is cold,
Like my shroud,
It is covering me till I can't be seen,
I cannot sway in the wind
To rid the snow.

One day soon,
I shall rot and be forgotten,
But my saplings will be noticed and cared for,
Till they become fine, proud trees
For children to climb on their strong branches
And to hold them safely.

Peter Shipway (9)
Penns Primary School, Sutton Coldfield

A Tree In Winter

My bark is very gnarled
Yet I feel so young, I am scared of it.
Children used to jump on my branches,
But now my branches are too frail,
Even the birds have flown away.

My once glorious leaves, crumble and fall in the powerful wind,
I wish I could still sway on my roots,
But the winter blizzards glue me to the ground,
How I still think about my young past.

I don't know what will happen to my saplings,
But my spirit has to be free.
I am waiting for my winter,
So I can pass away.

Pavan Bhambra (9)
Penns Primary School, Sutton Coldfield

My Grandpa

Grandpa's hands as soft as pillows
And his hair is like a bush
Skin is as gentle as silk
Really he is an inner child.

Grandpa's forehead is like unironed clothes
And his beard is a haystack
His nose is as red as a cherry
His eyes are small beads.

Grandpa wishes he could
Play football with me
But when he looks in the mirror
He sees his inner child.

George David Lowe (9)
Penns Primary School, Sutton Coldfield

The Old Wise Man

There once was
A very old man,
As wise as an owl,
But feeling as weak as any man can.

As frail as glass,
Sitting on his chair,
Rocking back and forth,
With a falcon's stare.

His wrinkles hold secrets,
Like a safe holds treasure,
His mind holds memories,
Beyond any measure.

He once was lively,
Prancing about and around,
Now he remains seated,
Without a sound.

Thomas Skidmore (9)
Penns Primary School, Sutton Coldfield

My Grandpa

Weary, old, like a crumpled up rug
He sits in his armchair, motionless
His hands are like twisted roots from the very first tree
But his inner child shines through like never before
The rippling veins are like rivers on a map
His hair shines like silver
This is my grandpa
Weary, old, tears like drops of dew
The war still tires him
The echoing gunfire haunts him
I love my grandpa!

Joshua Williams (9)
Penns Primary School, Sutton Coldfield

My Grandma

My grandma's name is Sue
She has skin like a scarecrow.

Balancing on her head
She wears a straw hat
With wild spaghetti hair
Sticking out.

She misses nothing
With her black, beady eyes
And she's the best grandma
In the *universe!*

Gemma Hutchinson (10)
Penns Primary School, Sutton Coldfield

My Nan

My nan is the world to me
She is very, very old
Her wrinkles round her eyes
Are like a crooked old tree.

Her face glowing, like light when she sees me
With sparkling eyes like silver stars
She gets weaker and weaker every day.

She has grey clouds of hair like candyfloss
Although she has skin as rough as a stone
When she smiles
She is like a young girl again.

Anisah Iqbal (9)
Penns Primary School, Sutton Coldfield

Someone To Remember

Skin, smoother than the first pebble,
You lie there doing nothing but sleeping.

Your few strands of hair,
Soft as silk.

Your sea-blue eyes,
Covered up by pale eyelids.
When you cry,
Pools of blue stream down your face.

Joseph Smith (9)
Penns Primary School, Sutton Coldfield

My Grandad

There is an old man called Daniel
Who lives on a farm, lonely and downhearted.
With wrinkled skin and bony hands,
He watches the world go by.

His grandchildren that live too far away
Sometimes phone him.
He wishes he could be with them always
He misses his family a lot.

Alexander Martin (9)
Penns Primary School, Sutton Coldfield

Old Lady

Veins in her hands
Are as blue as rivers
Her wrinkly hand is the dusty land
Her hair is the colour of the white, white snow
Wrinkles like the bark of a tree
Eyes bright green like emeralds
As soft to cuddle as a furry carpet.

Chloe Grigg (9)
Penns Primary School, Sutton Coldfield

Grandpa

Grandpa's hands are as red as blood,
There are marks where he's held his many guns.

Grandpa's eyes are as sharp as the falcon's,
From being on watch duty.

Grandpa's skin is as rough as shattered stone,
Where he had an accident in the trenches.

Grandpa's face is full of lines,
Each one telling a story of the war.

David-Jack Hanson (9)
Penns Primary School, Sutton Coldfield

My Grandad

Grandad's hands are as dirty as tree roots
But as warm and cosy as a winter fire.
His body is as old and frail as a scarecrow
His face is wrinkly
But full of kindness all over.
His eyes are full of trust and care
His hair shines like silver silk.
I love my grandad.

Sean Sheppard (10)
Penns Primary School, Sutton Coldfield

Old Man

Old man's nose like a strawberry,
Cracking beard as rough as straw,
Eyes as hard as stones,
His forehead is creased like un-ironed clothes.
He stumbles as he walks,
Limping up the stairs as slow as a snail,
His old bones creaking like broken stairs.

Keyron Facey-Price (9)
Penns Primary School, Sutton Coldfield

A Tree In Winter

Soon it will be the end of my life
Old people's hands are my twisted roots
My smooth bark has turned all rough with age
My branches are so weak
My leaves were so beautiful, that people would admire my beauty
But now they walk past like I was never there
When I was younger I could sway in the breeze
But now I will just fade away.

Jivan Badhan (9)
Penns Primary School, Sutton Coldfield

Old Man

A beard like haystacks,
Wrinkles as deep as roots in the ground,
A smile like the morning sun,
Pointed sharp nose like a carved stone.

Hands bonier than stone,
Eyes that sparkle like the stars,
Days flying by faster than ever,
Desperately trying to be like his inner child.

William Lai (9)
Penns Primary School, Sutton Coldfield

Winter Tree

I am nearly at the end of my life,
My bark is wrinkled and gnarled,
My branches are as weak as paper,
My leaves, no longer green.

When I was young I could dance
In the light of the moon,
I am at the end of my life,
Winter has come and I must go.

Olivia Mobbs (10)
Penns Primary School, Sutton Coldfield

My Grandma

My grandma has hair as white as snow
She still feels as young as 19
Her eyes are like rough, crumpled sacks
But you can still see that special twinkle in her eyes
My grandma is the best!

As my grandma moves, she's wobbly and weak
Her wrinkles sway too
Even though she is old and ancient
That doesn't matter
She is still my grandma!

Meena Hoda (10)
Penns Primary School, Sutton Coldfield

My Grandma

I love my grandma who is always kind to me
She gives me treats and sweets
And sits me on her knee.

My grandma has hair like a white fluffy cloud
When she smiles at me
It is a sunshine smile
Like a flower blooming
I love my grandma.

Amy Shaw (9)
Penns Primary School, Sutton Coldfield

Old Woman

Old woman's eyes like strawberries
And teeth like sparkling wine
Nose as flat as a pit bull terrier
She smiles, chortling to no one at all
Folds of fat wobbling around her chin
Her eyes glazed with happiness.

Nicole Price (9)
Penns Primary School, Sutton Coldfield

The Lighthouse

Lighthouses, lighthouses shine so bright,
In the darkness of the night.

I guide ships around a big rock,
Then they have a nice safe dock.

Lighthouses, lighthouses shine so bright,
In the darkness of the night.

People climb, climb so high,
Up a spiral tower the lighthouse won't let anyone die!

Lighthouses, lighthouses shine so bright,
In the darkness of the night.

Surrounded by a deep blue sea all ahead,
And a baby seagull going to bed.

Lighthouses, lighthouses shine so bright,
In the darkness of the night.

Hannah Farley
SS Mary & John's Catholic Primary School, Wigan

Day And Night

Running round having fun,
Hooray! Playtime has begun,
Playing tig with our friends,
I hope this playtime never ends,
What time is it? We don't care,
We'll have our playtime anywhere.

Everything's dark when you go to bed,
Scary nightmares lurk in your head,
When you wake up in the middle of the night,
Spooky shadows give you a fright!

Sally Dickens (9)
SS Mary & John's Catholic Primary School, Wigan

Summer Is Here

Outside in the hot sun,
Children playing games,
Footballs, tennis balls and lots of names,
Children playing with each other all of summer.

Adults come outside deciding to sunbathe,
Everyone outside enjoying themselves,
They get burnt and smack themselves,
Getting soaked with water.

People taking their dogs for a walk,
Frisbees flying everywhere,
Dogs confused never move anywhere,
Everyone out in the hot sun.

End of summer,
No sun shining,
People buying jumpers always lying,
Staying inside in their beds.

There is no hot sun.

Cameron Scott (9)
SS Mary & John's Catholic Primary School, Wigan

Dream

I had a dream, not any old dream,
A real horror dream too.

The monsters were hairy all spooky and scary,
I wish I always knew.

Pictures with eyes what a spooky surprise,
They give me the creeps too.

Chloe Jordan (8)
SS Mary & John's Catholic Primary School, Wigan

Dick And Dom The Dogs!

Dogs, dogs they are a pain,
Walking them, playing with them,
Feeding them,
Bark, bark, woof, woof.

But Dick and Dom the dogs,
Woof, woof, bark, bark,
TV mad like my dad,
Buying leads, buying feed.

Mischief mad, mischief mad,
Getting lost like my dad,
Woof, woof, bark, bark,
Mischief, mischief, mischief mad!

Matthew Brewder
SS Mary & John's Catholic Primary School, Wigan

Teachers

Mr Handly,
Is very manly,
He's got a loud voice,
And you have no choice.

Miss Jennings,
Likes to do her spellings,
She's very calm,
And she likes it to be warm.

Mr Wood,
Likes you being good,
He likes going fishing,
And he is always wishing.

Annabel Rowlands (8)
SS Mary & John's Catholic Primary School, Wigan

Autumn Leaves

The autumn leaves fall off the trees,
With a gentle plink.
While Sir Winter's breeze is coming,
People are having a drink.

Brush! Brush! Away with the leaves,
Into the bin they go.
So when you see them in the bin,
Run and shout, 'Oh no!'

Autumn leaves are nearly extinct,
Because it's winter season.
So be happy always,
Cos they'll come back if you leave 'em!

Mia Jones (9)
SS Mary & John's Catholic Primary School, Wigan

The Clone Wars

Slam! went the gunner,
Falling from the wall,
Bang! went the cannon,
Blowing up the sea.

'Help!' said Jango running,
From the army,
The army has attacked,
People had died.

Jedi protected themselves,
The Clones had won,
The droids had failed again.

Luke Chatterley
SS Mary & John's Catholic Primary School, Wigan

We've Won The Grand Final

We're drawing, we're drawing,
Who will win?
Five minutes to go,
We've scored a try,
So it's time to say goodbye,
For you to win,
It's in the bin,
We're the champions,
Hooray, hooray,
We've won!

Louis Fairhurst
SS Mary & John's Catholic Primary School, Wigan

The Old Chair

As black as a blackboard,
As ripped as can be,
As thick as a log,
As tall as a tree,
It's rickety and rackety,
Chittery and clattery,
But this old chair is still the chair for me.

Nichole Dennis (8)
SS Mary & John's Catholic Primary School, Wigan

Animal Mind

It's raining cats,
It's raining dogs,
It's raining all of the time.
It's raining bats,
It's raining frogs,
It's playing with my mind!

Dannielle Fisher (8)
SS Mary & John's Catholic Primary School, Wigan

The Beautiful Frog

Once there was a beautiful yellow and green frog,
In the middle of the woods sitting on a log,
With spots and stripes placed all around,
Ribbit, ribbit, he said jumping on the ground,
He was sitting under a bush wondering what to do,
He thought to climb a tree so he did and the rabbit hopped out, 'Boo!'
The frog and the rabbit had a game of tig,
'Oh you can't catch me, I'm the running twig,'
Frog was catching the runaway twig,
And Rabbit was catching Frog,
But once again he sat on that nice brown log.

Noah Gibson (8)
SS Mary & John's Catholic Primary School, Wigan

Music

I listen to the music pumping through my head,
I rattle with my pencil on the bars that led.

I thought through all the music that I like,
The wheels were spinning to the beat of my bike.

When I got to school I turned my iPod down,
I got into the classroom and pulled a big fat frown!

Beth McLelland (9)
SS Mary & John's Catholic Primary School, Wigan

Magic Footballs

Footballs are white,
Footballs are black,
When you kick a ball it
Comes right back!

Daniel Smith (8)
SS Mary & John's Catholic Primary School, Wigan

My Birthday Party

I have been to a birthday party,
It was so so fun.
We sung Happy Birthday,
When it just begun.

Chorus:
We had some crisps,
We had some cake,
We pinned the tail on the donkey,
It was totally fake.

We watched TV,
We played outside,
Somebody hurt me,
And they lied.

Chorus

It was soon night-time,
And everyone was asleep,
I went down stairs,
For a little peep.

Chorus

It was nearly morning,
And everybody was in bed,
'Wake up! Wake up!
You sleepyhead!'

Chloe Baybutt
SS Mary & John's Catholic Primary School, Wigan

Mr Crabs

Mr Crabs lives underwater,
Moving fast like a mad person snapping with his giant pincers,
Waiting to snap your fingers off,
When I go to the beach swimming in the sea,
Beware of Mr Crab and don't forget he likes money.

Chilambwe Chanda (8)
SS Mary & John's Catholic Primary School, Wigan

Under The Sea

Under the sea,
There are wonderful creatures,
And plenty of features,
Like a million fish before your eyes,
Under the sea,
What sort of things,
Are swimming with me?

Under the sea,
There are many divers,
And the angelfish are all stripy,
All of the crabs are trying to swim,
Then they see a dolphin fin,
Under the sea,
What sort of things,
Are swimming with me?

Jake Stephens (9)
SS Mary & John's Catholic Primary School, Wigan

The Beach

There go the children down to the beach,
All over the sand, in their mouths, in their cheeks,
Building sandcastles, paddling in the pool,
The beach is great especially when it's cool.

Seeing your footprints as you pass by,
And the seagulls as they fly in the sky,
Now crashing sandcastles, it's getting dark,
Coming back now, but someone's gone over the mark!

Conal Cunningham (9)
SS Mary & John's Catholic Primary School, Wigan

The Battle

I once saw a battle,
Where there were dead cattle.
The soldiers were hurt,
Most buried in the dirt.

There were lots of trenches,
Filled with some benches.
You could see the blood,
Buried in the mud.

Liam Burrows (9)
SS Mary & John's Catholic Primary School, Wigan

What Is A Book?

Books, books, ever to be found,
In the air and on the ground.
Some are thin, some are thick,
Some are sold very quick.
Read them in schools,
Read them in pools.
And that's what a book is.

Amber Tobin (8)
SS Mary & John's Catholic Primary School, Wigan

Clickity-Clack!

There goes the old smoky train,
Going through the countryside starting to rain,
Passing through stations like a bullet,
In a pond they saw a mullet.
Clickity-clack down the track . . .

Dan Williams (8)
SS Mary & John's Catholic Primary School, Wigan

Snow Fall Snow

Snow fall snow,
Come out children, come and play,
Lengthened night, means less time to play,
Every flake speaks bliss to me,
Falling so beautifully,
Wreaths of snow surround the town
People shouting to make plenty of sound.

Ashley Raju (9)
SS Mary & John's RC Primary School, Wolverhampton

Christmas Night

Leaves falling from the trees,
The snow is up to my knees.
The floor is white,
What a beautiful sight,
Not a bird in flight,
On this Christmas night.

Selina Peake (9)
SS Mary & John's RC Primary School, Wolverhampton

Winter Flake

Snowfall, snowflake,
The last snow, that falls on the floor.
I wish another, I wish for more,
I wish for a million,
To fall on the
Floor.

Dareece Wagstaff (9)
SS Mary & John's RC Primary School, Wolverhampton

Snowflake

Like a blanket of sand,
Coming from God's hand.

Has a big fall,
Falls like a ball.

It's very small,
Like a bouncing ball.

It always touches the ground,
Appears all around.

Such a beautiful sight,
It's there all night.

Only on a winter's day,
Beautiful like they say,
Never appears in May.

You can make snowmen,
But not a snow hen.

Callum Cartwright (9)
SS Mary & John's RC Primary School, Wolverhampton

Harvest Poem

Harvest is the tenth month of the calendar,
And we collect all the food for the elderly from farmers' fields,
And harvest is the tenth month of the year when we all cheer.

Harvest is the tenth month of the year,
My dad drinks dirty beer,
And all the kids play in the leaves,
All the squirrels collect their nuts,
And put them in their huts,
As the squirrels eat the nuts in their mouths,
We look at the sky and geese fly south.

Arron Steen (8)
SS Peter & Paul's Catholic Primary School, St Helens

The Thunderstorm

The thunderstorm's a big grey wolf ripping everything,
He knocks the dustbins over,
His tail sways side to side,
Looking for something to eat,
The roofs disappear, they've been eaten,
By the angry wolf.
He rushes through the city raging,
Ripping the trees, there's no forest left,
The wolf howls in the moonlight,
His eyes glow like coals,
He rushes back to his home,
Up in the grey mountains,
Rushing before it's too late,
Before the morning comes.

Sophie Williamson (10)
SS Peter & Paul's Catholic Primary School, St Helens

Green Is . . .

Green is the swaying grass,
Green is a colour of an apple,
Green is the colour of amazing leaves,
Green is a sad colour, not happy,
Green is the colour of petals on the flower,
Green is a horrible spell,
Green is a hopping frog in the blue water,
Green is the colour of a shiny lily pad,
Green is the colour of a big tall tree,
Green is an army, big and strong.

Joshua Eaves (8)
SS Peter & Paul's Catholic Primary School, St Helens

Red Is . . .

Red is the colour of
A beautiful red robin's breast.

Red is the colour of
Blood dripping from your veins.

Red is the colour of
Your shiny lips.

Red is the colour of
Your angry face.

Red is the colour of
A sparkly ruby.

Red is the colour of
A dragon.

Red is the colour of
Blazing fire.

Red is the colour of
Your sunburnt skin.

Red is your juicy apple.

Jessica Monnelly (7)
SS Peter & Paul's Catholic Primary School, St Helens

Pink Is . . .

Pink is a heart of love.
Pink is sweet candy.
Pink is a pair of glittery shoes.
Pink is a butterfly, soft and stripy.
Pink is the colour of a fairy's dress.
Pink is a hot Cadillac.
Pink is a hot lipstick.

Jodie-Lee Boardman (8)
SS Peter & Paul's Catholic Primary School, St Helens

Yellow

Yellow is the colour of a pillow.
Yellow is the colour of a go-kart.
Yellow is the colour of my favourite bobble.
Yellow is the colour of a shooting star.
Yellow is sickly and smelly.
Yellow is the colour of a dragon.
Yellow is the colour of sick.
Yellow is the colour of a newsletter.
Yellow is the colour of tingling bells.
Yellow is the colour of sand.
Yellow is the colour of paper.
Yellow is the colour of ice cream.
Yellow is the colour of chips.
Yellow is the colour of 'The Simpsons'.
Yellow is the colour of spicy curry.
Yellow is the colour of smoky teeth.

Rhianna Baker (8)
SS Peter & Paul's Catholic Primary School, St Helens

Red Is . . .

Red is fire, hot and painful.
Red is The Saints' rugby shirts.
Red is a strawberry, very juicy.
Red is anger on a face.
Red is a warning.
Red is a ladybird's skin.
Red is a shining ruby.
Red is a dragon's eyes.
Red is an apple, juicy and sweet.
Red is a tomato, very tasty.
Red is a firework, loud and noisy.
Red is Santa's clothes and sledge.
Red is Rudolph's nose on Christmas Eve.

Oliver Simpkin (7)
SS Peter & Paul's Catholic Primary School, St Helens

Why I Love Winter

I don't think the frost is nice,
Because then I slip on ice.
A sudden frosty breeze,
Blows the leaves from the trees.
Having a snowball fight is great,
Like building a snowman with your mate.

Without the birthday of Jesus,
There wouldn't be a Christmas.
When Santa comes at night.
He tries to stay out of sight.
He leaves the presents by the dozens,
For you and all your cousins.

Daniel Moore (8)
SS Peter & Paul's Catholic Primary School, St Helens

Green is . . .

Green is the soggy grass.
Green is the crinkly leaves.
Green is the colour of an apple.
Green is the swaying slimy seaweed.
Green is the colour of our amazing world.
Green is the grassy fields.
Green is the tasty lettuce.
Green is the leprechaun's hat.
Green is the colour of a spiky alligator.
Green is the slimy, hopping frog.

Jonathan Greenall (8)
SS Peter & Paul's Catholic Primary School, St Helens

White Is The Colour

White is the colour of a sparkling quilt of snow.
White is the colour of a clear glass of fresh milk.
White is the colour of the fluffy clouds in the sky.

White is the colour of Jesus' robe.
White is the colour of a soft tissue.
White is the colour of the happy seagulls.
White is a good colour to mix other colours with.

White with red makes pink marshmallows.
White is the colour of a clean sheet.
White is the colour of a healthy juicy bone.

Megan McEvoy (8)
SS Peter & Paul's Catholic Primary School, St Helens

Harvest Day

October is here,
We'll dance with joy,
We'll sing together,
Let's celebrate harvest day.

We'll share our food,
We'll be happy,
We'll care for each other,
Let's celebrate harvest day.

We like to play,
We like to talk,
We like to laugh,
Let's celebrate harvest day.

Ellena Owen-Moreno (8)
SS Peter & Paul's Catholic Primary School, St Helens

Harvest Poem

It's harvest time again,
The crops have grown with the help of rain.

It is time to pick corn,
We'll do it before dawn.

At harvest time we'll celebrate,
All the things we've grown and ate.

Wheat, corn, barley and hay,
Make a lovely dish today.

Harvest time comes around,
With the wheat that comes from the ground.

Lots of berries all around,
Squirrels crawling on the ground.

Joseph Whitfield (8)
SS Peter & Paul's Catholic Primary School, St Helens

Yellow Is . . .

Yellow is the colour of tangy lemons.
Yellow is the colour of tasty bananas.
Yellow is the shining pumpkin lights.
Yellow is the colour of a shining candle.
Yellow is a spicy curry.
Yellow is the autumn leaves.
Yellow is the colour of a felt-tip.
Yellow is a stripy buzzy bee.
Yellow is a sickly smell.
Yellow is the colour of ice cream.

Owen Jackson (8)
SS Peter & Paul's Catholic Primary School, St Helens

Fire Dragon

The fire is a dragon,
Swishing through the cave,
Devastating the land,
Searching for his prey,
Spluttering and spitting his poison to anyone,
Burning down the houses.

His tongue swishes and swirls,
His mouth opens wide,
He gives a loud roar,
He storms back down the city,
Back to his cave,
He lies down,
And waits until another night.

Megan Giblin (10)
SS Peter & Paul's Catholic Primary School, St Helens

Winter Is . . .

Winter is the time of year for snow and ice.
The berries are lustre-glossed.
The river is slow and has clinks of ice.
Geese fly south for the winter.
Trees are bare.
The leaves are crisp.
It is freezing cold.
We like to keep warm.
You can play in the snow for hours and hours.
I like winter season the best.

James Dean (8)
SS Peter & Paul's Catholic Primary School, St Helens

Old Age

Old age is bright red like a medallion.
Old age smells like the coast.
Old age tastes like the scrumptious tastes of Blackpool's burgers.
It sounds like a crackly sparkler.
It feels like wrinkled sheets that won't go straight.
Old age lives everywhere in the world.

Matthew Dixon (9)
SS Peter & Paul's Catholic Primary School, St Helens

Pink Is . . .

Pink is the colour of a pink squeaky piglet.
Pink is the colour of a lovely pencil.
Pink is the colour of a sweet pretty flower.
Pink is the summer, hot, cozy and warm.
Pink is the colour of a little butterfly.
Pink is the colour of a glittering heart.
Pink is the colour of a bright star.
Pink is the colour of a glittery feather.
Pink is the soft lovely rose.

Tyler Graves (7)
SS Peter & Paul's Catholic Primary School, St Helens

Green Is . . .

Green is the grass so gently cut.
Green is the leaves so brightly seen.
Green is an apply, juicy and sweet.
Green is a mint so cool and refreshing.
Green is an army so brave and strong.
Green is a frog, spotty and noisy.
Green is the background so beautifully still.
Green is a running routine.

Lee Hodgetts (8)
SS Peter & Paul's Catholic Primary School, St Helens

Red Is . . .

Red is the colour of your little cheeks.
Red is the colour of a juicy cherry.
Red is the colour of Snow White's big, juicy apple.
Red is a really big hat.
Red is an angry face.
Red is a tart, juicy melon.
Red is a surprised happy face.
Red is a big, beautiful butterfly.

Lauren Berry (7)
SS Peter & Paul's Catholic Primary School, St Helens

Green Is . . .

Green is the colour of the bright fields.
Green is the colour of leaves in the spring.
Green is the colour of a sour lime.
Green is the colour of St John.
Green is the colour of the sweet apples.
Green is the colour of a slimy toad.
Green is the colour of bushy broccoli.
Green is a nice bright colour.

Alice Fleming (8)
SS Peter & Paul's Catholic Primary School, St Helens

Yellow Is . . .

The taste of a juicy melon.
Yellow is a bendy banana.
Yellow is a blazing sun.
Yellow is a shining pumpkin.
Yellow is a colour of a dandelion.
Yellow is a hot and spicy curry.
Yellow is a colour of a person's hair.
Yellow is a bright light.
Yellow is a sickly smell.

Matthew Ross (8)
SS Peter & Paul's Catholic Primary School, St Helens

Orange Is . . .

Orange is a sweet tangerine.
Orange is a candlelit pumpkin.
Orange is the colour of Nemo.
Orange is the colour of a sunflower.
Orange is a carrot skin.
Orange is the colour of leaves in autumn.
Orange is the fierce colour for a tiger.
Orange is the nice taste of orange juice.
Orange is the beautiful colour of the sun.
Orange is the taste of crunchy cornflakes.

Heather Whittle (7)
SS Peter & Paul's Catholic Primary School, St Helens

Red Is . . .

Red is the colour of The Saints' clothes.
Red is the colour of Santa's snowy sleigh.
Red is the colour of multicoloured sunset.
Red is the colour of Santa's hat.
Red is the colour of Rudolph's bright nose in the night sky.
Red is the strawberries' juicy taste.
Red is the colour of hot soup.
Red is the colour of a dragon's eyes.
Red is the colour of squelchy tomato ketchup.

Amy Giblin (7)
SS Peter & Paul's Catholic Primary School, St Helens

Hope

Hope is a red and yellow flower.
It smells like fresh air up above.
It tastes like yummy food.
Hope sounds like a choir of angels.
It feels like my grandad kissing me.
Hope lives in all of my family's hearts.

Megan Lennox (10)
SS Peter & Paul's Catholic Primary School, St Helens

Harvest Poem

I'm lucky to be living in such a well off place.
When I think of other countries and the problems that they face.
I take it for granted that there's food upon my plate.
But in some places the weather can change a person's fate.
I think I'm badly done too if I can't have any sweets.
But what about the people who have no food for weeks?
Tonight I'll say a prayer to help their crops to grow.
Because I do care and I really hope they know.

Callum Leyland (8)
SS Peter & Paul's Catholic Primary School, St Helens

Blue Is . . .

Blue is the colour of dolphins' skin.
Blue is the colour of the school gates.
Blue is the colour of a whale,
Blue is the colour of a blueberry, juicy and sweet.
Blue is the colour of the light blue sea.
Blue is the colour of the light, bright blue sky.
Blue is the colour of Mary's jumper.
Blue is the colour of the world from space.
Blue is the colour of tears running down your face.
Blue is the colour of your veins.

Cameron Chester (7)
SS Peter & Paul's Catholic Primary School, St Helens

Happiness

Happiness is the colour baby-blue,
It smells like special chocolate,
Happiness tastes like fresh coconut,
It sounds like children's playful laughter.
Happiness feels like a new cushion,
It lives in a homey house.

Sophie Turner (9)
SS Peter & Paul's Catholic Primary School, St Helens

Harvest Poem

In harvest time the leaves fall from the trees,
And all the birds are flying in groups of threes.
Summer's sun is just like having fun.

When the birds fly it's so funny,
I could just cry when the flowers rise, they brighten up the sky,
When the stars and the moon rise up to the sky all around,
It's so funny when I try to reach the sky above me so high.
I could just cry when the cloud's have passed me by.

Reece Phillips (8)
SS Peter & Paul's Catholic Primary School, St Helens

Hate

Hate is a red beam in the dark,
Hate smells like burning,
It tastes like hot toast from the oven,
It sounds like the screeching from the guy next door,
It feels like flames that turn to ash when you talk of peace,
It lives in the dark dungeon of war at night.

Liam Sephton (9)
SS Peter & Paul's Catholic Primary School, St Helens

The Light Of Love

The light of love still shines,
It is as red as a rose,
It smells like fresh strawberries,
It lives in my dreamworld,
It tastes like candyfloss,
It feels like waves going side to side,
It sounds like birds singing in the distance.

Olivia Nelson (9)
SS Peter & Paul's Catholic Primary School, St Helens

Winter Poem

The trees are bare.
All the leaves are frozen.
The riverbank is frozen.
With clinks of ice.
Snowmen freeze with frosted ice.

My voice echoes in the winter snow.
My ears are cold.
People's feet slipping under snow.
Animals hibernate till spring comes again.

Rebecca Murad (8)
SS Peter & Paul's Catholic Primary School, St Helens

War

War is a deep red blood colour,
It smells like rotten dead bodies,
It tastes like sour sweets,
It sounds like punching and shouting,
It feels like a pain rushing through your body,
War lives in a castle, shut in a dungeon.

Jack Tickle (9)
SS Peter & Paul's Catholic Primary School, St Helens

Hope

Hope is the purple dusk,
It smells like sweet honey,
Hope tastes like a juicy apple,
It sounds like sweet singing,
It feels nice,
Hope lives everywhere.

Harry Ward (9)
SS Peter & Paul's Catholic Primary School, St Helens

The Orphans

There was once a homeless orphan,
Walking the streets with her brother,
When she was only young her father had died
and so did her mother.

She grew up to be nine,
Her brother eight,
But soon they will suffer their parents' fate.

She was looking paler one day, that girl Jenny,
She looked like a crisp white sheet,
Beneath her ragged clothes there was her belly,
And on her belly there was hardly any meat.

Jen's brother just the same, poor Code,
He looked as white as a ghost,
And to tell you the truth he was just rag and bone!

Whilst they were walking along one night,
They needed to cross the road,
She told her brother to stay there,
While she rescued a toad.

But alas, a lorry was coming!
Which the children did not see,
It was coming closer now,
And then it knocked them over,
And there lying on the ground,
Were two peaceful children.

No one noticed them not a single one,
But there in the morning the blood shone,
Walked on, stamped on and silent,
The orphans were . . .

Dead.

Bethany Beales (10)
SS Peter & Paul's Catholic Primary School, St Helens

Hope, Faith And Peace

(Dedicated to my grandad Harold that I love and still love now, because he sadly died on the 05/09/05)

Hope is peach likes baby's soft delicate cheeks,
It smells like fresh apples picked from the vine,
Hope tastes like tenderness strawberries,
It sounds like people laughing in a meadow,
It feels softer than silk,
Hope lives in every tree and every living person.

Faith is red like a heart beating,
It smells like fresh salad, just been brought out,
Faith tastes like vanilla ice cream, fresh and cold,
It sounds like children having fun,
It feels like a soft fluffy pillow,
Faith lives in our beating hearts.

Peace is yellow like the gleaming sun,
It smells like a lovely perfume just mixed,
Peace tastes like a pear just picked,
It sounds quiet and silence in the Earth again,
It feels like clouds floating by,
Peace lives in a green, grassy park.

Alexandra Hudson (9)
SS Peter & Paul's Catholic Primary School, St Helens

Love Is In The Air

Love is the colour of pink like a freshly picked raspberry,
It smells like fresh peaches,
It sounds like waves splashing lightly,
It feels like touching a soft marshmallow,
Love lives safely in my heart.

Daniel Byrne (9)
SS Peter & Paul's Catholic Primary School, St Helens

Yellow Is . . .

Yellow is the colour of a shining sun.
Yellow is the colour of 'The Simpsons'.
Yellow is the colour of the melons.
Yellow is the colour of tarty melons.
Yellow is a bright light.
Yellow is a spicy curry.
Yellow is the colour of chips.
Yellow is the colour of a speeding cheetah.
Yellow is the colour of a busy bee.
Yellow is a smell.
Yellow is the spotty frog.

James Picton (7)
SS Peter & Paul's Catholic Primary School, St Helens

Love Is . . .

Love is a pure white dove flying in the blue sky,
It smells like fresh strawberries being picked,
Love tastes like a fresh apple pie,
It sounds like lovebirds singing on the perch,
Love feel like a baby's cheek,
It lives in the middle of our hearts.

Katie Ascroft (10)
SS Peter & Paul's Catholic Primary School, St Helens

Fear

Fear is the colour of a dark tunnel,
It smells like mucky handprints,
Fear tastes like horrible liquorice,
It sounds like someone breaking into your house,
It feels like torture,
Fear lives at the bottom of my heart.

Danielle Barton (10)
SS Peter & Paul's Catholic Primary School, St Helens

Love For Everyone

Love is a pale pink like a slim flamingo,
It smells like the nicest perfume ever made,
Love tastes like a nourishing peach exploding in your mouth,
It sounds like a lovebird tweeting in the trees,
It feels like soft lips touching each other,
Love lives in all our hearts.

Ryan Briggs (9)
SS Peter & Paul's Catholic Primary School, St Helens

Feelings

Jealousy gets you nowhere,
You should be proud of what they have done.
It's like green slime,
It's like chicken burning in the oven,
It sounds like someone shouting down your ear
Telling you to stop being jealous,
It feels like rough, burnt hands,
It lives in the dark side of your heart.

Bekky Ann Livesey
SS Peter & Paul's Catholic Primary School, St Helens

Happiness

Happiness is a rainbow spread across the sky,
It smells like candles burning,
It tastes like a big bowl of magic,
Happiness sounds like people shouting as they play,
It feels like raindrops in the sky,
It lives deep in your heart.

Robyn Gaskell (9)
SS Peter & Paul's Catholic Primary School, St Helens

Red Is . . .

Red is the colour of an angry face.
Red is the colour of a bobble.
Red is the colour of a glass of red wine.
Red is a fire-blazing dragon.
Red is the colour of a book.
Red is the colour of a pencil.
Red is the colour of a red rose.
Red is the colour of a dragon.
Red is the colour of Santa's sleigh.
Red is the colour of Rudolph's nose.
Red is the colour of a red hat.
Red is the colour of your heart.

Chloe Hull (8)
SS Peter & Paul's Catholic Primary School, St Helens

Fear

Fear is blood-curdling red,
It smells like rubber burning.
It tastes like eating a hot curry when my mouth is burning,
It sounds like a bomb going off,
It feels like a dagger is in my heart,
It lives in a dungeon, deep and dark.

Adam Daprato (9)
SS Peter & Paul's Catholic Primary School, St Helens

Love

Love is bright red like a shining ruby,
It smells like Lacoste Red,
It tastes like red wine,
It sounds like a red car driving along the road,
It feels like people kissing that are in love,
It lives deep down in people's hearts.

Chris Cullum (10)
SS Peter & Paul's Catholic Primary School, St Helens

The River Of The Heart

The river is a horse of the heart,
The horse is galloping silky smooth downwards, downwards,
downwards into the sand.
Until dawn the horse gallops through the sand.
The horse's eyes gleam, gleam like the sun in the sky.
The horse's coat covered in water shining bright like the stars.
The night is dark and they melt into the sand.
Downwards, downwards, downwards into the sand.
The horses run into the dusk.

Laura Bailey (10)
SS Peter & Paul's Catholic Primary School, St Helens

Old Age

Old age is white like a sheet of paper,
It smells like Yorkshire puddings steaming on a plate,
Old age tastes like your Sunday dinner sitting on the table,
It sounds like the coughing of a bad chest,
It feels like a wrinkly sack,
Old age lives in an old sweet care home.

Ben Haggett (9)
SS Peter & Paul's Catholic Primary School, St Helens

Autumn

As I looked upon high,
I saw some birds fluttering by.
They fluttered high above the trees,
The branches were full of autumn leaves.
The leaves had turned to golden brown,
They swished and swirled as they came down.
The sweepers brushed and toiled away,
To keep the mound of leaves at bay.
And then at last the work was o'er,
The naked trees had leaves no more.

Lewis Johnson (10)
SS Peter & Paul's Catholic Primary School, St Helens

My Love Poem

Tell the surface of the water not to listen and not to make a sound,
Tell the birds to keep silent, a drop of rain to hit the ground,
Tell the plants not envy our love,
And kiss me gently,
As if the wings of a dove,
Do not tell my heart to stop beating, for it is filled with a bliss,
Do not tell me to close my eyes, just give me a kiss.

Jayde Farinha (10)
SS Peter & Paul's Catholic Primary School, St Helens

Different Colours

Blue is the colour of the lovely sky.
Blue is the colour of the big blue ocean.
Blue is the colour of a big shark.
Red is the colour of the Devil.
Red is the colour of blood.
Red is the colour of the Liverpool home kit.
Orange is the colour of a juicy orange.
Yellow is the colour of the sun.
Yellow is the colour of a banana.
Green is the colour of a big green apple.

Patrick Crehan (8)
SS Peter & Paul's Catholic Primary School, St Helens

Yellow Is . . .

Yellow is the sun shining on me.
Yellow is the colour of the book bags.
Yellow is the colour of juicy banana milkshake.
Yellow is a juicy lemon.
Yellow is the colour of the sand.
Yellow is the colour of a fish.
Yellow is the colour of an aeroplane.

Jordan Hutton (7)
SS Peter & Paul's Catholic Primary School, St Helens

Red Is The Colour Of . . . ?

Red is the colour of a car.
Red is the colour of a pen.
Red is the colour of history books.
Red is the colour of Liverpool's kit.
Red is the colour of card.
Red is the colour of a juicy apple.
Red is the colour of juicy strawberries.
Red is the colour of plump raspberries.
Red is the colour of design technology books.
Red is the colour of a burning fire.
Red is my best colour.

Luke McNamee (9)
SS Peter & Paul's Catholic Primary School, St Helens

Red Is . . .

Red is the colour of blood.
Red is an angry face.
Red is a colour of a pencil.
Red is a colour of a rose.
Red is a colour of Rudolph's nose.
Red is a colour of Santa's hat.
Red is a colour of a hot fire.

Ashlea Briggs (7)
SS Peter & Paul's Catholic Primary School, St Helens

Peace

Peace is glistening pink,
It smells like strawberries,
Peace tastes like chocolate mouse,
It sounds very quiet,
It feels very happy,
Peace lives in the heart.

Thomas Haggatt (9)
SS Peter & Paul's Catholic Primary School, St Helens

Yellow Is . . .

Yellow is the colour of the shining sun.
Yellow is the colour of the lights.
Yellow is the colour of a melon.
Yellow is the colour of the tangy lemon.
Yellow is the colour of chips.
Yellow is the colour of a cheetah.
Yellow is the colour of a triangular fish.
Yellow is the colour of a stripy bee.
Yellow is the colour of the warrior.

Ian Mark Moore (7)
SS Peter & Paul's Catholic Primary School, St Helens

Red Is . . .

Red is the sign of danger.
Red is the colour of a juicy apple.
Red is as juicy as a raspberry.
Red is the colour of blood.
Red is the colour of a bright cherry.
Red is the colour of a sparkling strawberry.
Red is the colour of a briefcase.
Red is the colour of a tomato.
Red's the colour of an angry face.

Kyle Ormrod (7)
SS Peter & Paul's Catholic Primary School, St Helens

Fear

Fear is deep, dark black,
It smells like a graveyard at night,
It tastes like burnt sausages,
It sounds like a sharp dagger digging into you,
Fear lives in a haunted house, locked in a cupboard.

Calum Briggs (9)
SS Peter & Paul's Catholic Primary School, St Helens

Red Is . . .

Red is the colour of a beautiful red robin's breast.
Red is the colour of your blood.
Red is the colour of your blood running down your veins.
Red is the colour of your shiny lips.
Red is the colour when you're angry.
Red is the colour of a sparkling ruby.
Red is the colour of a dragon.
Red is the colour of a blazing fire.
Red is the colour when you're boiling hot.
Red is the colour of a juicy apple.

Kenan Dyas (7)
SS Peter & Paul's Catholic Primary School, St Helens

Red Is . . .

Red is the colour of a burning fire.
Red is the colour of a robin's breast.
Red is the colour of a juicy raspberry.
Red is the colour of a person's death.
Red is the colour of a burning sunset.
Red is the colour of a juicy apple.
Red is the colour of the blazing sun.
Red is the colour of a dragonfly.
Red is my favourite colour.

Jack Kelly (9)
SS Peter & Paul's Catholic Primary School, St Helens

Love Is . . .

Love is peach, like people's skin,
It smells like fresh apples picked from the orchard,
Loves tastes like bread being baked,
It sounds like people laughing in the meadow,
It feels soft and squishy like a marshmallow,
Love lives in the top of our hearts.

Kathryn Ratcliffe (9)
SS Peter & Paul's Catholic Primary School, St Helens

Harvest Poem

Harvest is when the leaves fall off the trees and the berries are
ripe to pick.
The wind blows and when the geese go south the corn is golden
and the wheat is being harvested.

Harvest is when the wind is blowing hard and the birds are
gathering berries.
It is getting colder and the robins come out.
Animals start to find places to sleep.

It is nearly winter.
Squirrels are gathering nuts.
Birds are singing a happy tune as if they were so glad.
We are in bed all tucked up.
I cannot sleep because I am so excited it is Christmas Eve.

Jessica Berry (8)
SS Peter & Paul's Catholic Primary School, St Helens

My Rabbit Thumper

My rabbit Thumper is cute and fat.
His fur is very soft and silky.
He has a bushy tail.
His ears are pointy and very delicate.
He loves running around in the garden and he doesn't bite, he
loves jumping around.
He is the kind of rabbit to have and loves people.
I love my rabbit Thumper.
His coat is beige and brown.
His nose is very wet and his whiskers long and pointy.
He has two front teeth and they are very sharp.

Jodie Farrell (9)
SS Peter & Paul's Catholic Primary School, St Helens

The Wind

The wind is a howling dog,
Picking up litter into a whirlwind,
Hanging around street corners,
Sniffing in bins and boxes,
Howling at houses,
Wrapping around trees and bushes,
Speeding through windows,
And darting down streets.

The wind is a howling dog,
Rushing and raging around trees,
Staring at people,
Pushing them over,
Whipping up leaves,
And carelessly tossing them away.

Beth Reilly (11)
SS Peter & Paul's Catholic Primary School, St Helens

The Storm

The storm is an angry cheetah,
Weaving in and out of trees,
It sends its cold, damp breath,
Darting through the streets,
It lets out an angry roar,
Pounds angrily on windowpanes,
Its eyes flash across the dark sky,
As it gobbles up everything,
In its way,
And it lets out one last roar,
Before pounding furiously away.

Abigail McEvoy (11)
SS Peter & Paul's Catholic Primary School, St Helens

The Fire

The fire is a savage dragon,
Destroying everything in its path,
Gobbling up,
Everything in its path.

Chasing madly after its prey,
Killing off everything in its way,
Its enormous paws shaking the ground,
All are aware,
It's moving quickly now.

It prowls past the houses,
Burning all of them down,
Nobody can tell what it will do next,
The dragon is unpredictable.

John Foster (11)
SS Peter & Paul's Catholic Primary School, St Helens

The Sea

The sea is a beautiful horse,
Galloping down the beach.

White and dappled grey,
Its silvery hooves sinking, sinking
Into the sand.

With its silky white mane flowing,
In the wind.

And when the night falls and the
Tide comes in.

The beautiful wild horse gets
Down on the floor and is no longer
A wild horse but a beautiful
Sleeping horse.

Anna Garrity (10)
SS Peter & Paul's Catholic Primary School, St Helens

If I Were A Grown-Up

If I were a grown-up, I am glad to say.
I'd sit on the sofa and watch TV all day.

If I were a grown-up, I'd buy a flash new car.
A sports car or Mini, well maybe a Jaguar.

If I were a grown-up, I'd buy an enormous mansion,
In fact, something bigger, I'd have a vast extension.

If I were a grown-up, I'd make my life so good.
I'd even be so mad to down ten bottles of Bud.

But I am still a little child.
Well, I can still go mad and wild.

Sean Marsh (10)
SS Peter & Paul's Catholic Primary School, St Helens

The Snow Tiger

The snow is a beautiful snow tiger,
Creeping through the snow,
On silk padding paws,
It shakes glistening snow off its
Thick furry coat.

The snow feels cold on his
Soft leather nose,
Creeping through the snow,
Looking for his prey.

It cuts a hole in the ice,
Catches a fish,
After having its super,
It wanders home,
Into its small cave,
It calls home.

Amy Ritson
SS Peter & Paul's Catholic Primary School, St Helens

The Bull

The flash.
Maybe it was the bull.
The fierce bull waves its springy tail,
In the dark flames,
The eyes are murky,
The feet are blazing,
Because the bull has arrived!

Inside its cruel heart,
Unkindness burns,
Heavy, irregular toes,
Fungus-coated,
The stomach gigantic.
Black, lumbering body.

Wind howling through its empty head.
Horns too sharp to touch.
Its ears pricked,
Listening to conversations.
So beware of the ugly beast,
Beware! Beware! Beware!

Alison Cliffe (10)
SS Peter & Paul's Catholic Primary School, St Helens

The Spooky Witch

The witch flew past as the night wind howled,
With her long pointed nose she just scowled.
Her hair turning green and her big black teeth,
Lucky, her cat, watched from beneath.

She pranced about her fire and cackled,
Casting her spells whilst the fire crackled.
But really beneath all her casting spells,
Lies a kind-hearted witch in a castle with bells.

Holly Redmond Hopkins (8)
St Mary's Catholic Primary School, Crowborough

The Poppies' War

On the 11th day of the 11th hour,
There were guns going side to side,
Yellow corn and misty, dewy morn filled the atmosphere with fear,
Families were getting scared about the fathers who'd risk their lives,
Petals frail and roses fell,
The land was covered in black soot,
Clear and red and yellow beds,
We visit and remember their graves,
In all our hearts and dreams,
They will be with us once again,
We will always remember them.

Charlie Vousden (9)
St Mary's Catholic Primary School, Crowborough

The World In 60 Years

In 60 years' time the world will be black,
In 60 years' time a tsunami will wipe out England,
In 60 years' time robots will rule the world,
In 60 years' time the world will be on fire,
In 60 years' time the world will destruct,
In 60 years' time there will be a cloning machine,
In 60 years' time there will be a new sport called 'booty rugby football wars',
In 60 years' time a meteorite will hit Earth,
In 60 years' time Earth will vanish.

Oliver Crane (9)
St Mary's Catholic Primary School, Crowborough

Fireworks

They come in all different sizes,
And make all sorts of noises.
Some are big, the size of footballs,
But some are tiny like Christmas candles.

With lots of different colours they light up the sky,
Pinks and blues, greens and reds.
Yellow that looks like trails of gold,
And white bursts that look like thousands of stars.

There are lots of different sounds too,
Some screech upwards, whizzing and whirling.
Others make a big whoosh and then explode,
While a few go silently up and finish with a big *bang!*

They bring us pleasure on a cold autumn night,
Children gaze at them in wonder.
With an 'ooh' and an 'aah' we watch them perform,
But all to soon the excitement is over.

Megan Ryan (8)
St Mary's Catholic Primary School, Crowborough

Remembrance Day

Poppies for remembrance time,
They grow all through the year.
Bombs come crashing down,
And the soldiers disappear.

Their families hope they will survive,
Whilst the bullets fly.
Rotting flesh and threatened lives,
Many fighters fell and died.

Poppy Diver (9)
St Mary's Catholic Primary School, Crowborough

The Poppies That Grew After The War

There once was a poppy
That grew in a field,
It shed its seeds
All over the ground.

But grass spread over them
So they couldn't grow,
And they slept for a while
Down below.

One day came some soldiers
Who dug around,
Making trenches and shell holes
All over the ground.

Now the grass was gone
The poppies could grow,
They reached up for the sky
Like their mother had done.

So where the soldiers' blood had been
The blood-red poppies could now be seen.

Philip H Marshall (8)
St Mary's Catholic Primary School, Crowborough

When I'm Sixty-Nine

When I'm sixty-nine there will be 5D television.
There will be peace in the world and no wars.
Bombs and guns will be banned from the world.
No bad people to hurt other people.
And everyone will live forever.

Holly-May Penny (8)
St Mary's Catholic Primary School, Crowborough

Fireworks

Fireworks bang and flash in the sky.
They fly up really, really high.
They can be orange, green, purple and blue.
Listen to the crowd as they go, 'Whoooooo.'
All the children's sparklers are flashing.
To the noise of the fireworks crashing.
Catherine wheels are spinning fast.
While the rockets shoot up high and blast.

Dean Goldsmith (8)
St Mary's Catholic Primary School, Crowborough

The Haunted House Of Horrors

In the haunted house of horrors, in the dead of night,
I heard a strange and eerie noise, it gave me quite a fright!
Thought it might be Frankenstein, so I lay awake in bed,
I shook and shivered and shivered and shook from my toes
up to my head.
I got up very quietly just to make sure it was okay,
Frankenstein had left but I think he'll be back again someday!

Millie Coe (8)
St Mary's Catholic Primary School, Crowborough

Alexander

A lexander was a king
L auren is my sister
E ating I like
e X tra special
A t my house it is very noisy
N ot a lot of people are my friends
D isaster is my middle name
E aster I like
R ats I do not like.

Alexander Greig (10)
Strathburn School, Inverurie

Victoria

V ery vicious at times!
I love swimming and dancing.
C hristie is my *best* friend.
T oria is my nickname.
O range is my favourite fruit.
R achel and Morven are my other friends.
I love my family too!
A rt is my favourite subject!

Victoria Allan (10)
Strathburn School, Inverurie

Rebekka

R ebekka was at the beach
E very day was so sunny
B eneath the sand we go
E merald is my least favourite colour
K ind to people
K angaroos are so cute
A nimals are so cute too.

Rebekka Allan (10)
Strathburn School, Inverurie

Tamara

T ime to eat
A te my supper
M ake a cake
A re you hungry?
R oad signs
A re you happy?

Tamara Abel (10)
Strathburn School, Inverurie

Kayleigh

K ayleigh is my name
A spider fish stung me on the foot once
Y ellow is my least favourite colour
L ike to play Bratz dolls with Lindsay
E lle is my cousin's name
I like to play outside
G rapes are one of my favourite fruits
H ave you got a favourite?

Kayleigh Boyd (10)
Strathburn School, Inverurie

Ashleigh

A shleigh is my name
S chool is fun
H elping my mum
L ibra is my star sign
E very day I play with my friends
I love my family
G olden highlights
H appy girl.

Ashleigh Booth (10)
Strathburn School, Inverurie

Ryan

R eally like football
Y ells a lot
A ll 'The Simpsons' posters I have
N ever eats pizza.

Ryan Coutts (10)
Strathburn School, Inverurie

Valerie

V alerie is my name
A nne is my middle name
L ove my family so much
E llie is my friend
R ebecca is my friend as well
I really like to sing
E merald is my favourite colour.

Valerie Chapman (10)
Strathburn School, Inverurie

Melissa

M orven is one of my best friends
E llie is one too
L ovely kittens, I love so much
I have a sparkling personality
S onny is one of my cats
S o are Peachy and Pasha
A nd I love my family so much.

Melissa Cocker (10)
Strathburn School, Inverurie

Lauren

L auren is my name
A pet dog I have
U p all day to go outside
R unning is my favourite sport
E at a lot of scampi
N ever play football.

Lauren Bandy (10)
Strathburn School, Inverurie

Nicole

N ow I like to try new things
I have learned lots and like lots more things that I didn't used to like
C atching balls I like to do
O ranges are my favourite food
L ovely flowers I like a lot, they brighten up my room
E arth I like to preserve.

Nicole Gibb (10)
Strathburn School, Inverurie

Ellie

E veryone calls me Ellie
L ike Nicole and Christie
L ike the sun I do
I don't like it misty
E veryone else doesn't seem to like it either.

Ellie Huxtable (10)
Strathburn School, Inverurie

Martin

M agic gallery
A lways famous
R ight in the mansion
T o the paintings
I n the chair he reads
N o fire in the candles but ice.

Martin Inglis (10)
Strathburn School, Inverurie

Christie

C an you keep secrets?
H ow long does it take to tell?
R eally personal ones you have to keep
I could keep them all
S wimming is my hobby
T o swim is really fun
I like the smell of chlorine
E xcellent fun in the sun.

Christie Milne (10)
Strathburn School, Inverurie

Andrew

A lways golfing
N ever tired
D on't like fish!
R eally like football
E very day
W ant to play golf.

Andrew McGill (10)
Strathburn School, Inverurie

Ross

R ollerblading
O n the ice, skating
S nooker I play
S noring when I sleep.

Ross Michie (10)
Strathburn School, Inverurie

Rachel

R eally good for answers
A nd fab to play with!
C hristie, Victoria and Katy are my number one friends
H ey, I'm no angel!
E llie's also one of my friends
L azy, that's me!

Rachel O'Shaughnessy (10)
Strathburn School, Inverurie

Jordan

J oker Jordan
O n the ice
R olling down the hill
D ogs I like
A nd running's my sport
N ow you know all about me!

Jordan Paton (10)
Strathburn School, Inverurie

Jack

J ack, my name is
A mazing at the computer, I am
C ultured, I am a little
K nuckles, mine are *hard!*

Jack Neilson (10)
Strathburn School, Inverurie

Katie

K ind to all animals
A nthony won 'Big Brother' this year
T rampolining is my favourite sport
I went to Florida for my birthday and I went on all the fun rides
E lephants are so cute.

Katie McSwayde (10)
Strathburn School, Inverurie

Katy

K ind Katy
A lways an angel
T ries hard all of the time
Y ou do not know how lucky you are to have me.

Katy Ingram (10)
Strathburn School, Inverurie

Lindsay

L indsay is my name
I n class pay attention
N othing is the same
D o you think the same?
S am is annoying
A lways nice
Y oghurts are my favourite.

Lindsay Stanhope (10)
Strathburn School, Inverurie